URBANISM AND TRANSPORT

Helmut Holzapfel's *Urbanism and Transport*, a bestseller in its own country and now available in English, examines the history and future of urban design for transport in major European cities. This book shows how the automobile has come to dominate the urban landscape of cities throughout the world, providing thought-provoking analysis of the societal and ideological precursors that have given rise to these developments. It describes the transformation that occurred in urban life through the ongoing separation of social functions that began in the 1920s and has continued to produce today's phenomenon of fractured urban experience—a sort of island urbanism.

Professor Holzapfel examines the vital relation between the house and the street in the urban environment and explains the importance of small-scale, mixed-use urban development for humane city living, contrasting such developments with the overpowering role the automobile typically plays in today's cities. Taking insights gained from its historical analysis with a special focus on Germany and the rise of fascism, the book provides recommendations for architects and engineers on how urban spaces, streets, structures, and transport networks can be more successfully integrated in the present day.

Urbanism and Transport is a key resource for architects, transport engineers, urban and spatial planners, and students, providing essential basic knowledge about the urban situation and the challenges of reclaiming cities to serve the basic needs of people rather than the imperatives of automobile transport.

Helmut Holzapfel studied civil engineering, first working in leading positions from 1980–1993 as a transport scientist in research groups and later as an official at the Transport Ministry of North Rhine-Westphalia, Germany. Since 1993 he has been a professor at the Faculty of Architecture, Urban and Landscape Planning at the University of Kassel, Germany, and since 2009 has led the research project "Sintropher" in close collaboration with Sir Peter Hall. *Urbanism and Transport* was first published in German as *Urbanismus und Verkehr* and went on to become a bestselling book on urban and transport planning.

"A much-needed exposition of the appropriation of the street for the automobile—and an argument for the redesign of the inner connectivity of cities, with the person as the active agent."

—Robin Hickman, Senior Lecturer,
Bartlett School of Planning, University College London, UK

"Holzapfel offers a seasoned argument for a transportation policy oriented no longer toward a fossil-fueled mobility that increases speed and distance, but aimed at livable, vibrant urban structures. He offers a clear-eyed critique of conventional policies that have not only shaped cities but contributed to the problem of climate change."

—Michael Renner, Senior Researcher, Worldwatch Institute

"This is a fascinating book which provides refreshing new insights for English-speaking readers into the development of European urban transport and land-use planning and the role of the car over the last 100 years, from a German policy perspective."

— Peter Jones, Professor of Transport and
Sustainable Development, University College London, UK

URBANISM AND TRANSPORT

Building Blocks for Architects and City and Transport Planners

Helmut Holzapfel

Routledge
Taylor & Francis Group

NEW YORK AND LONDON

First published 2015
by Routledge
711 Third Avenue, New York, NY 10017

and by Routledge
2 Park Square, Milton Park, Abingdon, Oxon OX14 4RN

Routledge is an imprint of the Taylor & Francis Group, an informa business

Library of Congress Cataloging in Publication Data
A catalog record for this book has been requested

ISBN: 9781138798175 (hbk)
ISBN: 9781138798182 (pbk)
ISBN: 9781315756714 (ebk)

Typeset in Bembo Std
by Swales & Willis Ltd, Exeter, Devon, UK

Printed and bound in Great Britain by
TJ International Ltd, Padstow, Cornwall

CONTENTS

FIGURES

FOREWORD

Helmut Holzapfel's latest book has taken the debate around sustainable transport, urbanism, climate change, and the environment to an entirely new level: one that is long awaited and much needed. The last two to three decades have seen dozens of books about the illogicality and waywardness of transport trends. The trend for motorised transport can be summarised as a line on a graph starting in the bottom left-hand corner and going to the top right-hand corner, showing that we have more cars, drive more miles, have more trucks, and move freight over longer distances. This trend has been in evidence for many years and justified on a completely flawed understanding and analysis of transport based on equally flawed assertions about links between transport infrastructure and economic growth.

Holzapfel very ably and with great clarity demonstrates that an emphasis on mobility—as if more miles driven and more tonnes of freight moved around was intrinsically a good thing – is fundamentally flawed. He highlights the damaging consequences associated with the promotion of longer trips and shows that careful attention to urban form and structure and social interaction within a supportive legal and planning framework actually produces excellent places in which to live and work. He points to Tübingen and Freiburg as best-practice examples of the successes associated with modest, people-centred planning.

Holzapfel's book has emerged from a very clear scientific and philosophical German tradition. Germany has been at the vanguard of "automobility" for well over a century and its high rates of car ownership, miles of motorway, and rejection of speed limits on motorways show that Germany has grasped the Faustian bargain of more mobility with alacrity and enthusiasm. At the same time, Holzapfel is a leading representative of an impressive group of German transport and mobility critics who have shown that streets are for people, that "Tempo 30" (20 mph speed limits) create very fine living environments, and that high-quality places can be created. In spite of a century of automobility, Germany has nurtured a high-quality public transport system and more importantly has promoted the rather radical concept, unloved in the UK and USA, that urban planning, street design, and sustainability are all facets of the same thing, and civilised life prospers very successfully with low levels of car use and high levels of walking, cycling, and public transport use.

John Whitelegg, Stockholm Environment Institute,
University of York, UK

1

INTRODUCTION

Streets and Transport: Separation or Connection?

A book about urbanism and transport must take a new look at what separates and what connects in this field to deal with the relation between these two essential factors appropriately. At the very outset, it is important to note that this endeavour to shed new light on separation and connection has been written by a German in Germany. This fact of national origin shapes not only the content of the work but also its method. It thus provides the English-speaking reader with a perhaps unfamiliar view of a characteristically European manner of analysis, as well as examining the relation between the city and the automobile in the country where motorised vehicles were first invented: a country that continues to play a decisive role in their further development.

Separation has always been a feature of the city. Ghettos, streets for particular trades, quarters with mansions for the rich—much of this already existed in ancient Roman settlements and even before these times. Typically, the argument is made that the transport system should connect such disparate elements. Certainly, transport has played and continues to play this role. But, as the following will show, the manner in which this role is fulfilled varies depending on the type, speed, and extent of the transport provided. The separating function of a transport system has not been sufficiently analysed.

In this regard, one may only make reference to the classic works of Dieter Apel (prepared at the Deutsches Institut für Urbanistik, the German Institute for Urbanism, and unfortunately only familiar to the German public), in which this subject is extensively examined. A clear identification of these connecting and separating factors is, however, a necessary basis for establishing a relation between transport and urbanism. It is also the basis for integrating transport in a social consideration of the urban space, as undertaken for example by Henry Lefèbvre. His writings and the ideas found in the current works of Karl Schlögel[1] and Dieter Läpple[2] in Germany are scarcely to be found in academic works devoted to transport planning. But a spatial analysis of transport is essential if it is to be considered in terms of urbanism. At the same time, a consideration of transport planning is lacking just as much in the recent analyses of urbanism mentioned here. The present work aims to overcome these deficits and provide just such a synthetic view of the subject.

Also necessary for this undertaking is a short reappraisal of the various misunderstandings regarding the role of transport in history. One cause of these misunderstandings is the fact that many classic works about the development of the city were written in the phase of industrialism/Fordism, and the then new phenomenon of long-distance transport with its benefits for various parties was projected into the past (see Figure 1.1). In addition, an erroneous representation of the role of transport has often been made in recent years, with the debate very strongly orientated to the modern growth of long-distance transport. This book shall show that both of these influences have resulted in an overestimation of the relevance of long-distance transport to urban development. Clarification of the state of knowledge regarding the relation between space and transport is first necessary if we are to have any chance of making a realistic assessment of the current developments in this area.

The goal of this work is not only to overcome widespread prejudices regarding the role of transport and its effect on urbanism and the space of the city, but also to provide strategies for dealing with the current questions of urbanism that confront us today. In the contemporary discussion about "global" spaces, transport has indeed acquired a fully new function. In this connection, the thesis has been formulated that distance no longer plays a significant role in spatial relations because, for example, an e-mail sent from one point on the globe to any other point takes the same amount of time. On the other hand, space and distance do continue to exist, particularly in the everyday lives of just about all of us, where they persist in playing an important role. In current developments, however, this space has "shifted" in its accessibility and overall configuration in a manner that is unprecedented. In this regard, it is one of the consequences of modern forms of neo-liberal capitalism that new images of this space, various "maps", are continually being generated and overlaid on one another. This leads (often temporarily) to the creation of new centres as well as depopulation or demolition (e.g. abandoned industrial facilities or remote locations).

Most striking, however, and this will be the subject of remarks to follow, is the creation of what Karl Schlögel in a debate with Rem Koolhaas has called archipelagos.[3] These can be understood as spatial islands that are connected with one another by networks. Such spaces—self-contained residential areas, enclosed holiday resorts for the rich, secured communities as found for example in South Africa—are increasingly becoming the norm, in Europe and in many cities. The prominent art curator Roger Buergel described it this way: "Today in an English city, Indian workers live in the same area as the former English working class. But the two groups are nearly as far removed from each other as in the 19th century."[4]

There will and must always be social differences and contradictions, and these are expressed in many cases through segregation. Transport contributes significantly to this fragmentation of urban areas. Of course, transport supports the networks connecting Indian workers in an English city with one another, but these are different networks from those used by the English workers. Transport also separates residential areas effectively and very simply through the main corridors and thoroughfares that can hardly be crossed. The English authors Stephen Graham and Simon Marvin describe this as "splintering urbanism"[5] without succeeding in clarifying the role of transport in this process. As will be shown in the following pages, settlements and regions are becoming socially segregated, splintered units organised in separate communication networks.[6]

A work that deals with urbanism and transport and the current questions of further development must take on this situation as one of its starting points. It must also trace the history of the street—which was once seen as a useful amenity and has now become a distinctly unappreciated entity—and not only by protest-minded citizens' groups. An important undertaking of the future, which also has a societal dimension, could be to reconnect and reintegrate the archipelagos in urban (and suburban) space. A central contradiction of the post-modern period is without question a deficiency in groups of all sorts to deal with conflicts constructively, or even to recognise the living conditions and problems of a group other than one's own. A common sense of humanity and the development and enhancement of

FIGURE 1.1 The railway brought distant destinations "close" to one another for the first time in history (image: Jan Houdek)

cultural forms can only occur through direct personal contact and discussion. The continuation or the recovery of a capacity for urban integration would depend on establishing bridges between the archipelagos; this could be a new, trendsetting task for urban and transport planning. Thus an important aim of this book is to develop ideas and planning proposals for dealing with the "archipelagised", fragmented city and to provide useful input for current urban and transport planning activities.

Notes

1 The work of Karl Schlögel is not well known outside Germany. A translation of parts of his main work "Reading Time through Space: On the History of Civilisation and Geo-Politics" is provided by the Goethe Foundation at www.litrix.de/buecher/sachbuecher/jahr/2004/raumelesenzeit/leseproben/enindex.htm (accessed 30 October 2014).
2 See Läpple, D., "City and Region in an Age of Globalisation and Digitisation", in: *German Journal of Urban Studies* 40 (2001).
3 At the "Interview Marathon" with Rem Koolhaas and Hans Ulrich Obrist on 5 May 2007.
4 So-called "gated communities".
5 Cf. Graham, S., Marvin, S. (2001).
6 In this book, the very widely used and often misunderstood term "communication" appears for the first time. In the following it will not be used for the exchange of senseless noise, but rather (for example in the sense of Flusser, 1998, pp. 12–13) as a process for the creation and exchange of differences, thus as a "negentropic process".

2

WHAT WE THINK ABOUT TRANSPORT AND URBANISM

Mobility: A Culture and Phenomenon of Industrialisation

It might seem that it is outside the purview of a scholarly work to consider what our notions and ideas regarding transport are. One could assume that what really matters with such an eminently practical issue as transport is not what we think about it, but rather a physical reality, a set of things and systems in the world. However, such an assumption regarding the analysis of locomotion in our society could hardly be more misplaced.

The modern movement of persons and goods can only be explained and understood if we also look into the minds of the people using such systems. Even if this fact is often overlooked, transport is, in its essence, a cultural phenomenon, a product of the mind, which develops in any specific situation from a particular perspective. Transport planning and transport behaviour (including, of course, the purchase of a particular type of automobile) depend on an image, an idea in the minds of people—which is often quite far removed from reality.

Indeed, the relative rigidity of transport systems in the face of significant changes in the world comes partly from the fact that this is an area where little reflection takes place. When the present work begins with a consideration of the images in our minds regarding transport, it is expressly with the purpose of establishing a reflective relationship with the people (the cultural actors, as it were) in the area of transport.

Attempts to place transport in an integrated relationship with people and human culture in general have been made only rarely in the past. Many may even ask what the two have to do with each other. Transport is judged to be simply a technical factor with which we are confronted. This in any case has been the attitude found in planning activities over many years. Separated in official planning processes from its most important accompanying issues—namely, how we live in and plan our settlements—and even more from the question of what transport might ideally offer to people in their efforts to live together, transport has been handled as an isolated issue for decades. Therefore it is indeed unusual that this book investigates the question of what the continual growth in the movement of people and goods really has meant for our common life—particularly in urban areas.

In approaching the question of the images we carry in our minds regarding transport, it is first essential to look at the terms being used. How we think is, of course, influenced by the terms we use, and often we don't pause to examine the history of such terms. The terms "Verkehr" (transport or traffic) and "Mobilität" (mobility) used today in Germany in public debate have a central significance in the current culture, but only a relatively short history in the manner they are now used.

In the nineteenth century in Germany, the word "Verkehr" was used principally to refer to the interaction of persons with one another in exchange or social relationships. It was only in 1900 that the word acquired its current meaning of the transport of goods and persons. It was so defined for the first time in the Brockhaus encyclopaedia in 1909. Thus we see that the term "Verkehr", so important today in German parlance, first acquired its current meaning in the Wilhelminian period. The term "Mobilität" does not even appear in the first German dictionary published by the Brothers Grimm, the "M" volume of which first appeared in 1885 in the addition prepared by M. Heyne. With the word "mobile", one most probably thought of the military, which might be mobilised in the sense of being put in a "ready to march" status. The term "mobile" as used in Germany today was apparently derived from the final two syllables of the word "Automobil". This occurred first in the 1970s and took on the meaning of driving around in a car. The Duden Dictionary of Foreign Words published in 1974[1] translates "Mobilität" only in the sense of mental agility, the frequency of movement from one domicile to another, or movement between social groups (sociology). Even today, a clear definition of the term is lacking. In the field of transport, mobility typically refers either to the frequency of daily trips (probably by automobile) or the number of kilometres an average person travels in a year. Other proposed definitions—which certainly would be of more intellectual value—such as that proposed by Eckhard Kutter (viz., mobility is the ability of persons to reach the largest possible selection of different potential activities or facilities in a given amount of time) have not come into general use.

In any case, the term mobility acquired enormous popularity very quickly and was used in Germany particularly by the automobile club ADAC to push back against the growing strength of the environmental movement. This finally went so far that at the beginning of the present century there was a serious and intensive discussion about whether a "right to mobility" should be included in the German constitution, as the law professor Michael Ronellenfitsch repeatedly demanded, meaning mobility in connection with the automobile.[2] Indeed, one could begin to think that it simply hadn't occurred to mankind over the millennia that they had a basic human right to driving from here to there: Freedom, equality, fraternity, and. . . driving around?

This curiously evolved concept of mobility plays a central role in discussions of transport not only in Germany but also in the international context. Frequently, it is not even asked who, in fact, should have such a right to mobility. Thus Dietmar Kettler[3] has posed the provocative question of whether a basic right to mobility should not also apply to children and teenagers, who typically get around on foot. Automobile-based mobility is almost always associated with greater benefits, more understanding among people, and a higher level of prosperity. That there could conceivably be too much mobility is seen as an absurd hypothesis. Even many persons involved with environmental protection see the extensive movement of goods and people as a desirable phenomenon, to be limited only by the amount of energy consumed in doing so. Wolfgang Sachs' history of the automobile[4] is one of the few works of cultural history that examine how this perspective came to be established, but it deals with the aspect of transport planning only peripherally.

Only in connection with tourism (for example, Enzenberger's work already published in 1958) are there well-elaborated endeavours to pursue the question of what one gets from all this travel. In transport research, on the other hand, and also in city planning and urbanism, this subject is not dealt with frequently. Carl Benz, one of the inventors of the automobile, was one of the few who confronted this question. In his opinion, the unlimited distribution of his new creation would be a dreadful development. The Swedish geographer Thorsten Hägerstrand likewise posed the question in the 1970s of whether unlimited mobility really made sense. What influence people really could or should have in the whole matter, what role our humanity or our feelings can play: these questions have had no real traction in transport research. Transport psychology occasionally takes up such questions, but is more concerned with the reactions of car drivers in various traffic systems and considers the significance of mobility in the minds of the people only in rare instances.

With this prevailing approach, the dependence of what we think about transport and urbanism on our current historical situation does not become in the least bit clear. Today's form of transport with ever greater distances and international networks is, however, a phenomenon of the modern age and a conception of the culture of modernism, which has its roots in the Middle Ages.[6] But here, as is so often the case, many people believe that a discrete historical phenomenon will persist indefinitely and has always been so.

The famous Swiss historian Jacob Burckhardt devotes a chapter in his "Reflections on History" to the ludicrous egoism of judging everything that is similar to our own current state of being as happiness, and furthermore to project such similarities into the past and future.[7] An example of such behaviour is to define the twentieth-century concept of "mobility" as a basic human necessity, indeed as so essential a part of human existence that it is desirable to incorporate it in the German constitution.

A good example of the status of the current debate as conducted in politics, banks, and the mainstream of public life was provided in a speech by the former Berlin senator Thilo Sarrazin, who has incidentally dealt with transport policy professionally for many years: "As shown in the everlasting and constantly growing cult of the leisure individual with the car and the boat and the plane and skis and sport shoes and every other possible means of locomotion, this propensity is deeply implanted in our brain stem and cannot be rationally questioned."[8] If one contemplates this further, Sarrazin's remarks about the necessity of driving around more and more seem increasingly ridiculous. Something the inventor of the automobile found not at all desirable is deemed to be "deeply implanted in our brain stem", indeed "everlasting": humanity's constant motion on a mass basis.

In his work of cultural analysis on the development of the "love of the automobile" already mentioned above, Wolfgang Sachs shows how the values and terms connected with the rise of the automobile first developed. Not only the terms "mobility" and "transport" themselves, but also other accompanying concepts that are hardly more than 100 years old: Notions such as "speed" and "record" first became popular in the second half of the eighteenth century, while terms such as "arterial road" or "traffic flow" first came into being towards the end of the Second World War.

It is the express intention of this work to refute the many prejudices we carry with us, grounded in our way of seeing the world, which cumulatively amount to a belief that the type of locomotion predominant today and the ways people deal with time and distance constitute a kind of eternal truth. Such a perspective leads then to an uncritical acceptance by a supposedly well-informed public of undocumented and demagogic assertions such as those quoted above from the politician Thilo Sarrazin.

Mental images develop and continue to exist in our minds only when they find some sort of correspondence and confirmation in the complex social, material, and psychological processes of reality. The beginning of these processes, however, occurs principally in the "world of ideas" as can be seen in the development of the automobile and transport. Thus it was that the autobahns in Germany came into existence even though there were not nearly enough automobiles to fill them.

To demonstrate the load-bearing capacity of an autobahn in 1938, for example, it was necessary for the young transport engineer Bruno Wehner (who after the Second World War came to occupy one of the most important professorships in the field of transport studies) to bring together *all* of the available vehicles in the area of Frankfurt and Darmstadt to conduct his tests. But we are concerned not only with visions but also with reality. Without the social acceptance and high social significance accorded to mobility and transport in our societal value system, the continuing visions of ever higher levels of mobility could not be sustained.

It is not a natural instinct for mankind to be constantly in motion with externally propelled means of locomotion; it is one aspect of a particular form of life in modernity. The author of these lines introduced the concept of a distance-intensive lifestyle into German transport planning at the beginning of the 1990s.[9] Lifestyles and ways of living are not only a description of a particular sociocultural situation; it is also sometimes difficult to break out of such patterns, particularly if the society is organised in accordance with them. In organising transport, it is not only a lifestyle but also a whole cultural form having to do with prestige and power that determines specific perspectives, concepts, and possibilities of change. It is a moving moment when a new government minister insists on having a Jaguar as his official car, as recently occurred in Austria.

Weaker identities make gains particularly when they are able to demonstrate the unceasing necessity of their presence in all possible locations through the use of airplanes, helicopters, or expensive automobiles. The urge to ubiquity, to be present at all times in all places, shapes our age. That this has to do with power and dominance is evident in the practices of dictators or kings. Their images have to be hanging in all locations, particularly in official offices where citizens should follow their edicts. Nowadays, the lowly subject waits for the big man rushing here or there in a helicopter or a Lear jet—typically with the wish to switch roles if that were only possible. It is no accident that the travel arrangements of politicians are repeatedly the focal point of public scandals, which in fact have far greater causes. But the travel is what most readily evokes envy. The urge to mobility is a manifestation of modernity that carries a very high emotional charge.

In human history there have been times and places in which a strong emphasis was placed on overcoming great distances. But there have also been peoples, regions, and historical phases that were more orientated towards proximity, as Rudolf Wendorff's still impressive book *Time and Culture: A History of Time-Consciousness in Europe* shows.[10] The basic development of the city in Europe, for example, was without doubt a period when the focus was on handwork, small cultural units, and the local environment.

Likewise, in the interplay of urbanism and transport, our minds and the ideas inside them determine what is planned and considered. The assumptions about transport and the permanence of current attitudes regarding space and time remain unstated in the process of making concrete decisions. The current debate regarding the city and globality presupposes a range of assumptions about transport, which are not explicitly stated. These "tacit preconditions" and their history must be examined in more detail.

The Relationship Between Urban Development and Transport

In the general relationship of spatial development and transport, this book concentrates on the interplay of urbanism and transport. Urbanism will be defined as a comprehensive science of city development and life processes that also includes the social and economic conditions belonging to these phenomena. The word "urbanism" has a long history of being used in this sense in connection with city life. A well-known and oft-quoted reference is made to the term "urbanitas", used by Cicero to characterise a witty and indeed urban form of rhetoric and behaviour.

As in the case of transport and mobility, in which all judgements seem already to have been made, the public debate regarding the question of urban development and its interaction with transport appears to have reached an end and to be entirely clarified and complete. The generally accepted and continually repeated conclusion goes like this: The most important factor for urban development is the available long-distance transport connections, which trump all other determinants of urban development. While the history of proximity and its role for the city in transport planning and urban sociology are neglected, the generally accepted judgement regarding the significance of long-distance accessibility has virtually no documented support in the field of transport studies. Rather, these opinions are buttressed by an overly simplified interpretation of urban history connected with a number of primitive economic assumptions.

In the following we will take a closer look at these assertions. In the process, it will become clear that the argumentation for this view lies in the decisive role given to transport by nearly all relevant works in the complex processes leading to the emergence of the city. According to this view, the city develops basically through the effects of long-distance transport and large trade routes. If this was the case historically, the argument goes, then it must also be so today. A number of these arguments will therefore be inspected more thoroughly in this work.

The basis of these theories of city and urban development is the assumption that long-distance transport accessibility is if not the single then certainly the most significant factor for the initial development of cities. The present-day significance of transport for the city is deduced from this "well-known" fact. On the websites of many German cities, directly following mention of the fact that the city developed on an important historical trade route, one finds the further remark that its present-day position is close to a major autobahn exchange, representing a positive development factor.[11]

This common view of the development of cities is also to be found in the layman's account on the German Wikipedia: "The urban functions such as trade with other regions or serving as a central location for a rural hinterland demand the best possible connection of the city with its surrounding area. For this reason, most cities were founded at carefully selected locations, for example at the intersection of already existing trade routes, at river crossings or protected sea harbours."[12]

This entry deserves closer consideration. Without any particular differentiation or exact documentation, images from today or from the industrial period are "transported" into the past. The centrality theory of Walter Christaller is combined with the functional theory of the city that arose in the middle of the last century. This occurs even though these theories were developed to describe completely different circumstances occurring at an entirely different time—namely much later than the initial development of the city.

In the scholarly literature, the views presented are considerably more sophisticated. However, neither in urban nor in transport planning are there documented findings regarding the interaction of urbanism and transport. Even prominent authors in the field make do with suppositions and historical assumptions.

Lewis Mumford is certainly an author who set scholarly milestones with his reflections on the history of technology and the city. His statements about the modern destruction of the city through transport ("worship of speed") are illustrative of his criticism of the concept of mobility. In his classic work about the city,[13] the village plays an important role in the city's formation. The city is embryonically present in the village. In a further elaboration of his argument, influences from the village mix together with other culturally different factors coming from without.[14] This leads to a phase of urban development that extends over a longer period of time. The city is determined through a local, highly diverse collection of persons; this "urban mix" is what makes it successful. For Mumford, long-distance transport does not create the city; rather, it is the reverse: The city allows transport over greater distances.[15]

In other well-known "classics" of the field, for example the work of the Italian Leonardo Benevolo from the 1970s, long-distance transport does not give rise to the city. Benevolo develops a kind of interaction between village and city to explain the city's development. He writes about the first cities in the Near East: "Through the intensive agricultural activity, more food could be produced as was required in the country. The surplus of agricultural production was concentrated in the cities and allowed a continual growth in the urban population. This made it possible for the cities to develop handicrafts, trade and services which in turn supported growth in the agricultural production."[16]

According to Benevolo, it is the "added value" coming from agriculture that makes the formation of cities possible. Not much is to be found in Benevolo's work regarding transport routes. The first streets and routes in his maps, in fact, serve to make connections within the settlements themselves and points in the immediate vicinity.

The overestimation of the role of long-distance transport found in many popular accounts today may also be the result of oversimplified interpretations of archaeological results. It is certainly the case that the discovery of a locally produced fruit at an excavation is not nearly as interesting for the archaeologist as a piece of jewellery from some distant locale that was "untypical" of the region being investigated. The "untypical" was thus the interesting factor, and it came from far away. Long-distance travel and transport over great distances, however, were more the exception than the rule for many centuries—also for cities. This was so even if, as in the Middle Ages, such transport did result in extra profit for certain cities and strengthened their position, as with the cities belonging to the Hanseatic League, for instance. The formation of cities "through long-distance transport" can be assumed only in exceptional cases (for example, in locations such as oases or places of accommodation near mountain passes).

Against this background, it appears very questionable whether the initially cited and supposedly indisputable findings about the connection of city life and transport really have any basis. Examples of what has been written in internationally prestigious works about the connection of the city's development and transport show that speculative and empirical material must be brought together to make any statements at all about this matter. Nonetheless, there is hardly any convincing documentation for the prominent role of long-distance transport in the formation of cities that is to be found in many sources and in the popularly promoted view. In the following, a methodological approach for a more differentiated approach will be briefly presented, which while perhaps not explaining more can at least show how an integrated consideration of urbanism and transport might look. On this basis, various components of a more comprehensive consideration of urbanism and transport will be demonstrated and discussed.

A Few Hypotheses and Methodological Approaches to Clarify the Relation Between Urbanism and Transport

Persons and Space

As already stated, time-space representations of cities or settlements with an urban character are a rarity. Definitions of urbanity or the city often entirely neglect spatial aspects and reduce these to a point on the map to which characteristics are assigned. Insofar as spatial aspects are brought into the picture (particularly in geographical works), this then occurs in the dimension of metrical distances or in the context of spatial considerations with an economic basis, as in measurements of transport costs. In his *Essay about Space*, Dieter Läpple[17] characterises such concepts as "container space", making reference to François Perroux. In opposition to this notion, Läpple proposes a concept of "matrix space" as the starting point of a theory of societal spaces. With this approach, Läpple comes closer to an understanding of space such as that used by Henri Lefèbvre in connection with the city and urban conditions.

In our subsequent remarks here, an attempt will be made to understand space in its role as a factor of "socially conditioned production, appropriation and exploitation". That means concretely that urban relations will not be seen in accordance with their functions for a "total city system" but rather will be placed in relation to persons acting in specific situations and their corresponding social conditions. The human relationships in this connection, of course, also correspond to trade and exchange relations—in this regard, the causes and origin of products and the process of their creation become interesting. The city as a trading point on an arterial road can only be properly understood if the persons residing there with their various needs and ways of living, dressing, and nourishing themselves are also taken into account. This quickly transforms a "trading point" into a spatial object—with environs and social relations that also play an important role. In addition to the oft-mentioned "long-distance transport", there are then other completely different and just as interesting forms of communication that come into our field of view.

What Is the City, What Are Urban Conditions? Regarding the Object of Analysis

The various—and indeed there are many—definitions of the city or urban conditions show that it is not simple to exactly describe the object that will be at the centre of our further analysis. In many instances, in the relevant sources there is not even an attempt to define the actual subject to be addressed. This is certainly one reason why many theories of city development contain a sort of circular argumentation: If cities developed as trading points on long-distance routes, then they are also defined through this characteristic. Conversely, whatever develops in some other manner is simply not a city.

More exacting scholarly considerations of urban settlements that have been available for more than 100 years show a much more complex picture. As an example, we can turn to the analyses of Max Weber.[18] These are particularly interesting because in many cases they are enlisted (albeit without very close reading) by authors as justification for their view of the city exclusively as a transregional trading point. Indeed, the role of urban settlements as "market centres"[19] does appear at important points—particularly in the first pages of Weber's text. However, he makes little or no reference to long-distance trade. The simple statement "not every market shapes the locality" shows that Weber argues in a highly discriminating way. On the same page, he states even more clearly: "We wish to speak of the 'city' in the economic sense only when the local population satisfies an economically significant portion of their everyday needs in the local market, and indeed, do this in large part with products which the local population and the population of the immediate vicinity have acquired for sale on that market". The city is defined spatially as part of a settlement and the central point of the surrounding countryside. The locality gains its significance through the products of the "immediate vicinity". Those who render Weber as the chief witness for the significance of long-distance trade for the development of the city have in all probability failed really to read him.

Nor does Weber limit himself to economic definitions. In the further course of his text, other important manifestations of urban forms of settlement appear in a variety of descriptions. There is, for example, the "agricultural centre" made up of inhabitants who meet their food needs mainly or entirely from their own land.[20] This form of settlement, Weber explains, is typical for the cities of antiquity. He describes "special forms" of cities such as the "fortified city",[21] or entirely different forms of cities as in Japan. In his historical remarks, Weber also identifies completely different types of development to which urban forms of life can lead. As a consequence, one can see that it is necessary to consider far more various influences, including cultural factors and aspects of political power, to understand how a city comes to and continues to exist.

This is also the point at which the very incisive, if also highly complex, description of the "revolution urbaine" by Henri Lefèbvre[22] begins. This approach provides a basis that will be used in the material that follows. Like Weber, Lefèbvre also explains the formation of the city mainly in terms of the relation of the city and the countryside, in which he sees the occurrence of a domination by the "political city" over the surrounding area. In this process, Lefèbvre does not see trade as the decisive force in the dominance of the state, but rather administration and organisation. For him, trade constitutes only a single rather subordinate point of this order. In this connection, Lefèbvre introduces the term "heteretopia", making reference to Foucault.[23] Shortly and simply stated, the city contains very diverse, contradictory possibilities for activity which also include elements in opposition to the dominant moral order. For Lefèbvre, trade is also initially more of a "heterotopic" activity that assumes a dominant character only in the Middle Ages with the "commercial city".

Throughout, it is clear that Lefèbvre judges local administrative and organisational activities and the possibilities emerging from these as the determining factors in city formation. Beside this phenomenon, heteronomy represents the capability of urban organisation to tolerate contradiction: to realise change through diversity.

It is thus not without good reason that Lefèbvre directs his attention to the street, local exchange, and organisation. With the growing role of long-distance transport, this place (the urban street) tends to be increasingly disturbed. Thus an interesting thesis of Lefèbvre's is that long-distance transport and increases in trade have the effect of inhibiting city development rather than promoting it.[24]

Cities are thus defined as places of diversity and a locally functioning capacity for change. This is an entirely different aspect on which to focus than the city's accessibility in long-distance transport.[25] In the following, this idea will be reviewed and analysed in a number of different areas. The following hypotheses will be employed:

a) The role of internal, small-scale communication in urban settlements and their direct surroundings is typically underestimated—in relation to both past and present forms. Such small-scale networks are the basis for the city's diversity and the existence of contradictory elements and "counter-realities", which are important for evolution and renewal.

b) As small-scale communication has taken on an increasingly reduced role in modern transport theory, less reference has been made to persons as active agents in the urban context.

c) Well-established patterns of interaction between transport and settlement have developed in the course of history that ensure well-functioning small-scale communication in urban spaces. These patterns have often been disregarded in the last century in the establishment or alteration of cities or urban neighbourhoods.

d) In contrast, great attention has been paid in the past century to large-scale, long-distance projects of development for urban situations, which have a very different effect and function than local or regional development. This role will be more closely considered and examined here.

e) On the basis of these analyses, various conclusions will be drawn regarding the connection of space and transport in current urban situations. Significantly different focal points for the connection of urban development and transport than those found in current political practice can be derived from these conclusions.

Notes

1 Cf. Duden Fremdwörterbuch 1974, p. 469.
2 Cf. Ronellenfitsch, M.; Holzapfel, H. 2000, pp. 16ff.
3 Cf. Kettler, D. 2005.

4 Cf. Sachs, W. 1998.
5 Cf. Enzensberger, H. M. 1958.
6 Cf. for example Sloterdijk, P. 2005, pp. 38ff.
7 Cf. Burckhardt, J. 2007, p. 955.
8 Thilo Sarrazin: "Bemerkungen zur zukünftigen Finanzierung des Verkehrs aus der Sicht der Länderhaushalte". Statement at the conference of the Managers' Circle of the Friedrich-Ebert Foundation, "The Future of Transport – Financing and Mobility", on 22 November 2006 in Berlin.
9 Cf. Holzapfel, H. 1997.
10 Cf. Wendorff, R. 1980. Unfortunately, this was never translated into English.
11 The website of the small Sauerland city Olpe as just one example: "Es werden die bekannten Fernwege ... gewesen sein, die Entstehung, des Haupthofes, der Kirche, des Dorfes und später auch der Stadt Olpe bedingt haben ... Heute sind es die Autobahnen A 4 ... und A 45 ..." (from the website of the city of Olpe, accessed 29 October 2014: www.olpe.de/standard/page.sys/389.htm).
12 Cf. http.//de.wikipedia.org/wiki/stadt, accessed 7 September 2007.
13 Cf. Mumford, L. 1963, p. 21.
14 For Mumford, these are influences coming from the hunt; the exact way in which these "hunters" influenced city formation remains rather vague. Cf. Mumford, L. 1963, pp. 35ff.
15 Cf. Mumford, L. 1963, p. 33.
16 Cf. on this point and in the following: Benevolo, L. 1983, p. 22f. Although Benevolo has a basically positive attitude towards functionalistic approaches to planning, it thankfully does not occur to him to make "long-distance transport" an active agent as an abstract term in the formation of the city. He sees the city resulting from practical (agricultural) work and the surplus value that results from this work.
17 Cf. Läpple, D. 1992, pp. 157–207.
18 Cf. Weber, M. 1922, pp. 923ff.
19 Weber, M., p. 924.
20 Cf. Weber, M. 1922, p. 930.
21 Weber, M., p. 932.
22 Cf. Lefèbvre, H. 1972. The expression "revolution urbaine" refers to the changeover from originally village-based forms of human organisation to urban forms. The orientation in Lefèbvre's work also comes from contact with Klaus Ronneberger and his writings. Cf. Ronneberger, K. 2010.
23 Cf. Foucault, M. 2005, p. 10f. This approach of Foucault's, which unfortunately was not further developed by him, is quite impressive and provides important stimuli for city planners who are orientated towards Marx or Hegel. The city can, if it always includes its dialectical opposite, be "open" to further changes and new transformational processes.
24 Cf. Lefèbvre 1972, p. 14f.
25 Other authors have also been aware of this. Peter Hall, for example, in his magnificent anthology *Cities in Civilisation* (1998), begins his final sentence: "Cities were and are quite different places ...". Similarly, cf. Saskia Sassen (2006, p. 167), who also points to diversity as a distinctly positive element in today's metropolitan centres, as well as Lucius Burckhardt 2004, p. 108.

3

HOUSE, STREET, NETWORK

Small-Scale Organisation and Urbanism

The Role of Small-Scale Spatial Relationships

When we begin with the description of spatial relationships in cities by looking at small-scale forms of everyday use of space, this is not by chance. These forms of spatial use not only have a significant effect on the spatial relations in which people grow up, they also have a critical role in our tradition and history, and in the immediate social experience and contacts that shape our lives in general.

In the years between 1970 and 1980, various authors dealing with the subject of environmental psychology such as Lenelis Kruse in Germany[1] and Leanne Rifkin in the USA[2] had already pointed out the close connection between spatial arrangements and social relationships and learning processes. They are part of a tradition of earlier works from the fields of psychology,[3] philosophy,[4] and also sociology[5] that identified a considerable if not determining dependence of human development, mentalities, and social systems on the manner in which the spatial environment is organised.

To be sure, these various works make reference to very different structures and related structural details. For example, there are a large number of works including historical treatments that deal with the influence of the inner organisation of the house on the social relations and forms of communal living. The following pages, in contrast, will focus on the interaction between the house and the street, which of course can be affected by the inner form of the house, but our focus will be on the interaction itself.

The Street and the House in the Settlement

The layout of cities—the arrangement of the streets and houses or other buildings—has a considerable and often quite underestimated influence on human life. This is a very concise summary of the debate surrounding space and the city that occurred in the 1970s and has lately been resumed. Culture, forms of communication and confrontation, the transmission and generation of knowledge: these are all phenomena that are related to the small-scale organisation of buildings. At this point we can already state that the success of densely populated forms of settlement in the city depends just as much on the inner, small-scale quality and organisation of the city's streets and buildings as it does on the city's connection to the surrounding area and distant locations.

In the following, we concentrate on the orientation of buildings and the general connection of streets, the space around buildings, and the built structures themselves. This concerns the smallest, constitutive relation that shapes the connection of urbanism and transport. This has long been neglected in many analyses and in the actual practice of building because the exit from a house or the entrance to a building is the border between two disciplines (namely, architecture and transport planning). The interior of a house—on this subject there exist numerous works—is assigned to architecture and internal social organisation, and thus separated from what happens "outside", on the street and in traffic and transport.

The larger unit of street, forecourt, and built structures, the overarching analysis of "indoors" and "outdoors" (as Georg Simmel has demonstrated in the case of the door in his essay *Bridge and Door*[6]), is essential for a thoroughgoing understanding of urban organisation. The question addressed here is the orientation of a house to that which stands before it, a public space—or to put it differently, the decision concerning where a door should be situated. These elements of the organisation of human habitation have been an object of consideration for many years and an increasingly important part of how daily life is structured in the city.

In this connection, we find an interesting etymological overlap in the Old Testament (apparently going back to early linguistic formations of the Akkadian language): The front side of a tent (panu/panatu) is the same term as that used for the face of a person or of Moses; similar linguistic roots are also found in verbs such as "turn away" or "flee".[7] The physical orientation of structures for living was thus brought into relation with social and physical situations from a very early time, indicating their basic relevance for a range of everyday relations.

It is not our intent to present the complete history of the interaction of the house and the street. The rules and the process of developing a relation between the public and private spheres are highly complex and to describe these phenomena for European culture alone would go well beyond the scope of this work.[8] What interests us in connection with the organisation of exchange and transport are processes that are important in the relationship between the house and the street; these involve on the one hand separation (by the door) and on the other commonality and interdependence. Examples will be presented in the following.

In the Greek and later Roman city there already existed a highly developed system of rules for the arrangement of streets and buildings. Dense communal living in localities, particularly in Rome, made clear separations and distinctions essential. The rules that developed over time represented a sort of "civil code written in stone". Walls, doors, and borders prescribed certain forms of behaviour and made clear the relations of dominance and dependence. And it was precisely these borders that created and preserved a basis for exchange and trade.

In this process, complex forms of property rights and social hierarchies developed that corresponded with the existing forms of social organisation. Paul Veyne[9] makes reference to Vitruv,[10] who in his discussions of the intersection of public[11] and private in architecture always also includes the social aspects.[12] The clarity (and severity) with which social relations were regulated in the Roman city can be seen in an edict displayed at the main entrance of a house: "Any slave who leaves without being commanded to do so by the lord of the house shall receive 100 lashes."[13]

These were clear and emphatic limits that, as can be seen, would be enforced with drastic measures when necessary. The street itself also displays borders and hierarchies. In Pompeii (see Figure 3.1) a linear partitioning and orientation can be seen in the form of the street. The building entrances and sometimes complex transitions from public to private in the form of shops on both sides, a pavement, and a separated roadway create a clear linear hierarchy.

We do not know, of course, exactly to what extent these rules had practical effects. But the success of the Roman organisation of cities over time under highly variable and conflicting circumstances speaks for the relative effectiveness of the basic forms of the street that had been developed. Even after the end of the Roman Empire, the basic arrangement of street, forecourt, house remained in place in villages and cities, albeit in a much more simplified form. Here we should remark that the juxtaposition of the house entrances on both sides of the street

FIGURE 3.1 Street in Pompeii (photograph: author)

promoted small-scale communication across the street and beyond and thus the small-scale exchange of information. Through traffic in the contemporary sense of intercity long-distance transport was an absolute exception. Everyday processes were affected by such transport only to a limited degree.

The detailed organisation of city streets, which was first resumed in France and then spread gradually throughout Europe in the modern era, was very similar to the original Roman organisation. The unit of the house/street again took on a complex form as can be seen in an example of the typical Gründerzeit organisation of the street dating from the late nineteenth to the early twentieth century in Germany (see Figure 3.2). Such a form challenges us to provide an overarching interpretation.

In his essay *The Street as Free Space*, Karl Heinrich Hülbusch describes the street as a series of places that have been arranged in a row.[14] With this view he brings the small-scale exchange between "outside and inside" into the focal point of his considerations. Indeed, the typical Gründerzeit street is an example of how with a few simple, clear, and easy to understand rules a multitude of possibilities for human activity can be established.

The basis of the organisation of the street is once again the juxtaposition of building entrances.[15] In this way, the "view across the street" and then also the "way over the street" is directed to a destination on the other side of the street. Many authors, most impressively among them Jane Jacobs,[16] have pointed out the usefulness of the organisation of the street for regulating people's everyday activities and

FIGURE 3.2 Gründerzeit street in Kassel, Germany (photograph: Swen Schneider)

the small-scale exchange that accompanies such regulation. The role of the pavement, the function of the front yard of houses, or the means and effect of the linear orientation of the street are described in many sources that document the quality of street organisation and need not be mentioned here in detail. Empirical analyses in contemporary cities with similarly arranged streets, for example by Donald D. Appleyard, show that such streets with multiple pedestrian crossings over the roadway are used intensively for processes of exchange and interaction as long as automobile traffic does not inhibit or preclude such activities (see Figure 3.3).[17]

The symmetrical partitioning of the street and adjacent domiciles with house entrances, front yards and pavements (often also with a row of trees), and the roadway in the middle—a model that was designed in the nineteenth century in Europe and elsewhere—promotes comprehensible spatial relations and provides all concerned with a high level of security. At the edge of the street, from the door and the windows of the houses as well as the front yards, one can observe what

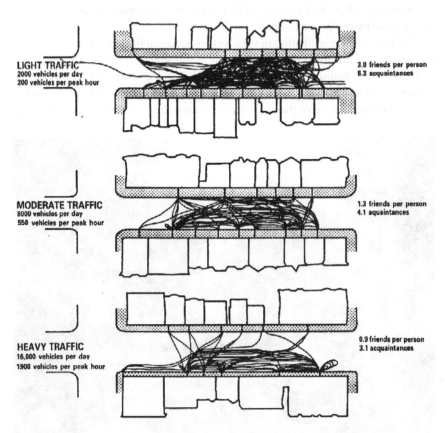

LIGHT TRAFFIC
2000 vehicles per day
200 vehicles per peak hour

3.0 friends per person
6.3 acquaintances

MODERATE TRAFFIC
8000 vehicles per day
550 vehicles per peak hour

1.3 friends per person
4.1 acquaintances

HEAVY TRAFFIC
16,000 vehicles per day
1900 vehicles per peak hour

0.9 friends per person
3.1 acquaintances

FIGURE 3.3 The higher the traffic load on a street, the lower the quality of life for residents living on that street. This is reflected in the reduced number of friendships and acquaintanceships between people living on the street (diagram: John Whitelegg based on Donald Appleyard)

is happening and attend to some tasks if necessary. The further one advances to the "middle", the more public and "risky" the situation becomes—with the kerb of the pavement marking the border to the exceedingly dangerous realm of the automobile.

A pattern of building in line with the course of the street corresponds with this model. The width of the street and the height of the adjacent buildings are in direct relation to one another. The quarters in the east of Bremen, Germany, with a distance of 14 to 18 meters from house to house across the street and predominantly three-storey structures, provide a typical example of this approach. With relatively small dimensions but good organisation, there is sufficient room for front yards and exterior space. This works in the city of Bremen with a density of population that is achieved in other regions only through the use of high-rise structures. With highly flexible architectural approaches, the buildings themselves display a very diverse set of uses from "normal" residential buildings to professional offices to small-scale workshops for building and other trades.[18] Altogether, this produces an area of mixed use with simultaneous high population density.

The Gründerzeit street is to be found in many different forms and of course not only in Bremen. Sometimes, for speculative reasons, buildings of six or more storeys have been built (as for example is still to be found in large parts of Vienna). This has the effect that a direct connection to the street is missing not only for the higher storeys of the adjacent buildings but also for the structures within the block. The width of the streets is too narrow in relation to the height of the buildings, resulting in a paucity of natural light at street level. In the back courtyards of Berlin, the living conditions were often deplorable because the population density was simply too high.[19] The city and its urban streets were thus also a place of misery and poverty. The construction was typified by the exploitation of the involved workers and speculative machinations by the dominant real estate actors. An idealisation of the era is not appropriate.

The streets of the Gründerzeit city—some commentators speak rather idyllically of the "European city"[20]—were a location never without conflict and confrontation. The point rather is that the conflict—even when it had a speculative origin—could take place in the urban locale itself. The streets survived a wide variety of situations, providing the people who lived there with diverse possibilities of use in accordance with simple and understandable rules.[21] From families with a high number of children in flats that by today's standards are far too small to professional offices or the demands of a communally shared flat, everything was and remains possible. A high-rise residential building from the 1950s—even if it happens to be painted differently in later years—will always remain a residential building (in the context of functionalised zoning, it could in any case not be otherwise).

The orientation of the houses to the street results in a high level of security for the users of the structures. This means observation by people rather than by cameras and closed-circuit television. But that is not the only effect. Exchanged looks of this sort are also a basis for understanding. The field of "strollology", developed by Lucius Burckhardt, examines in detail what happens when people walk through an urban setting and puts a strong emphasis on people's perspectives and forms of observation. The forms of contact and looks that are exchanged on a Gründerzeit street have a direct character and a different meaning in the minds of the persons who are looking. The view of a resident of a high-rise building over the city (or of a Google Earth user from a virtual helicopter high above the landscape) yields different thoughts and conceptions regarding the actual and social significance of the constructed world than what comes from real contact on a city street. These different types of perception are not to be characterised simply as "good" or "bad", but the difference in perspective most certainly has a considerable effect on the image in our minds regarding a given city (see Figures 3.4 and 3.5).

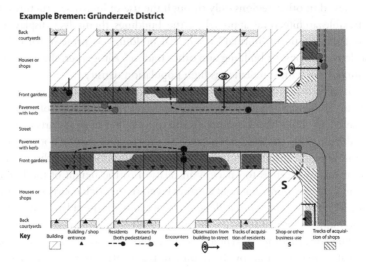

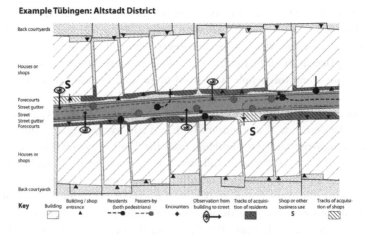

FIGURES 3.4 and 3.5   Tracks of presence and acquisition in compact, mixed-use urban neighbourhoods (drawing: Czekaj, T., Stratmann, V.; in Holzapfel H. et al. 2004, p. 51)

This leads us to consider the intellectual environment of urban planners who have aided and abetted the devaluation of communication in the urban street through the automobile in the past century. As we proceed, it will become evident that they promoted this development through one of two approaches—either by widening streets with a simultaneous devaluation of the adjacent structures or through a kind of defensive action in which the "bad through traffic" was displaced and diverted by various mechanisms, resulting in the sealing off of particular streets or entire sections of the city. A good example of this is provided in the work of Donald D. Appleyard, who seeks to liberate certain "restricted traffic" areas of the city but is forced to redirect the traffic elsewhere, thereby splintering the city all the more. The effects of such planning reactions go well beyond the particular streets in question. It is therefore necessary for us to move beyond an examination of the history and development of the street itself to consider the street network and the overarching connections.

Street Networks and the Intersection

It is certainly the case that the grid network used so successfully in the Greek and later the Roman city was not—as was once maintained—a "discovery" of Hippodamus of Miletus,[22] although he may have been involved in the building of impressive examples of such street networks. The inherently limited reach of the everyday relationships and contacts allowed by a single street makes it advantageous to connect one street to another to the extent that this is geographically feasible, and thus a grid is created. The concept of the Greek and later the Roman cities, which still shapes the form of many cities (and not the worst ones) throughout the world today, has demonstrated advantages of this concept over long years of use.

The grid system gives rise to many intersections. In addition to the relation of "being opposite" (from one side of the street to the other), the proliferation of intersections form a natural point of convergence and a sort of "joint" between individual streets. It was once again Jane Jacobs who pointed out the necessity of having shorter blocks and more intersections in the contemporary city (in the example of New York), thus emphasising what should be highlighted here: the advantages of the intersection.[23]

A crossing of ways brings together many possibilities—particularly from the standpoint of the pedestrian. I can, for example, choose different ways to reach the same destination. With a quick glance down the several different streets that open up, one gains orientation. An intersection also creates a point at which throughgoing traffic must slow down and residents may (and indeed must) make particular use of their right to cross the street—if they don't happen to turn at the corner. The intersection marks a point at which the opening up of an area affects the residents of that area. The residents note who is passing by; local interests ideally are well represented at such a point. The example from Pompeii (Figure 3.1) shows how clear structural markings (as a sort of forerunner of today's pedestrian crossing) secure these rights of the residents. The intersection is an ideal point for observers—such as the classic urban idler—as well as for other institutions. Bars and retail establishments are ideally situated on corners because of the multitude of passers-by.

The proper length of a block and the distance between intersections in a well-organised city cannot be generalised. In major cities, the blocks are larger than in smaller localities; in the course of history, these sizes vary. In the Middle Ages the grid-based organisation of the city was replaced with a more closely meshed, relatively unordered-seeming form that nonetheless continued to be typified by intersections and meeting points. Then at the latest in the nineteenth century, the grid-based city was once again established in a clear form. In European cities a block length of between 60 and 250 meters has predominated over centuries and is still to be found, for example, in the city centres of Freiburg or Bremen,[24] whereby larger dimensions occur infrequently. Street networks of this sort, which have been successful for centuries not just in Europe, typically have only two classes of streets: smaller access streets and main thoroughfares. A mixed-use approach for the buildings located on these streets was the generally accepted policy for a long time. This produced a pattern of streets in street networks roughly until the 1920s that was typified by a high degree of permeability.

From a place of residence, the city dweller had multiple possible routes of access to a wide range of destinations.[25] The dead end was an absolute exception, implemented only in extreme situations. Living on a street with people passing by gave a distinctive quality—streets were interesting. They were a meeting place and a source of information about what was going on in everyday life. The "window to the street" with the face of an elderly person at a window observing the urban situation with a cat asleep beside them may be a romantic image, but it says a great deal about a particular historical experience.[26] For a long period, the street was an attraction before this characteristic was forfeited—not only because of heavier automobile traffic but also because planners no longer took this into account when designing houses.

The two types of streets—the main thoroughfare and the smaller "normal" street—differ in their location, width, and the buildings to be found along them, although pronounced differences in all these characteristics are not always to be found. Businesses depending on walk-in customers, such as shops and restaurants, are found in the main thoroughfares. In the network these streets are often extensions of intercity connections and/or connected with a central square. The people of the city mainly live in the many smaller streets of the various city neighbourhoods.[27]

Particularly in the Gründerzeit period, elaborate grid networks developed in European cities. In Bremen, for example, many of the principal access streets have short distances between intersections—which continues to make such situations interesting for businesses today. An important result of the establishment of grid networks, particularly because they are usually limited to the two street types mentioned above, is that they promote a relatively even distribution of traffic through the city.

This does not result in an absence of conflict among the various possible uses of the city. In the city of the Middle Ages with its small-scale, mixed-use character, Thomas Sieverts, for example, already detects signs of persons being strongly

disturbed by the activities of business, and he judges the absence of such disturbance as an advantage of what he describes as the "in-between city".[28] Whether
such an argument is really convincing, when automobile traffic produces more
disturbance than many types of business, remains unclear. What is indisputable,
however, is that for a long period of time—and more than today—the city was the
place in which a great diversity of conflicts occurred and were worked through.

In such a situation, the gridded settlement organisation produces many good
results. The small-scale organisation of localities in the form of a grid not only
provided a space for conflicts over a long period of time, it also allowed people
the freedom to develop appropriate rules—an arrangement that often functioned
well. Of course, phases of overuse and overcrowding through speculative forces
did bring such organisation to the limits of what it could bear. But in many places
and in many historical periods, and also under contemporary conditions with a
modern portfolio of business real estate, the grid network demonstrates its positive
qualities. The city with many intersections is not only pedestrian friendly, it is also
in most instances an attractive locality—depending on many other parameters in
addition to this one.[29]

With the intersection, conflict is in a certain way built into the locality. Whether
it is pedestrians or automobiles that are regulating their rights of way, these are
moments that must be agreed on by a range of participants and actors because at an
intersection space is at a premium. The rules and patterns that develop in this context, however, are simple and clear. Even today at many intersections, traffic flows
better without a traffic light than with one. Certainly, intersections were never
romantic locations in a city and they often brought on conflicts and confrontations—
for example, in Germany in the street battles of the 1920s. But at the same time
they function as a local "hinge" in the mechanism of urban life.

Separation, Disintegration, and Displacement: The Strategies of Industrialisation in Transport

Since the Second World War (at the latest), everything has changed in the planning
of streets. Intersections are not desired and efforts are made to eliminate them. In
many treatments of the changes occurring in cities in the course of the previous
century, changes in the transport network are often disregarded and the effect of
these changes is undoubtedly underestimated.

Background

The small-scale organisation of urban localities was hardly still a subject of discussion in the main phase of industrialisation in Germany and Europe before 1900.
The last in-depth planning works on this subject already focused more on issues of
design.[30] In this area, ideas about urban development were based practically on the
experiences of the past. These experiences, however, were increasingly taken for
granted and thus had started to deteriorate as a basis for planning.

The opening up of the cities by the railways[31] also transformed the significance of the urban environment as a whole. The rail lines separated parts of the city from the surrounding countryside, and specific sections of the cities themselves were changed radically. The intrusions into existing urban life are comparable to what results from the construction of an urban highway today; in some instances, these intrusions extended into the very centre of the cities. Today we have grown accustomed to such extensive encroachments in our environment through construction activities. At that time, the effect on the sensibilities of the persons concerned was certainly enormous. That these projects could nonetheless be realised is only explicable when we consider the fascination and intense admiration the new machines provoked in the people with their powers that so enormously exceeded those of humans and animals. In addition, the economic growth in Europe from approximately 1850 to 1910 that accompanied this mechanisation was without doubt an impressive phenomenon that promoted acceptance of the changes taking place. Important population groups from the upper classes and particularly the urban elites orientated their conceptions of the future on the basis of images that came from this increasing mechanisation.[32]

The euphoria to be found in individual groups and the resultant willingness to make sacrifices in connection with development efforts can be compared—without stretching the historical comparison too far—with the situation in China today.[33] The changes that came with the development of rail transport were indeed remarkable. Following the opening of the line from Paris to Rouen and Orleans in the year 1843, the poet Heinrich Heine called the railway a "providential event"[34] and compared it with the invention of printing and gunpowder. His well-known quotation, "I feel the mountains and forests of all countries advancing towards Paris. Already, I smell the scent of German lime-trees; the North Sea breaks on my doorstep", gives an impression of just how deeply these developments affected the populace of the era.

In addition to the impact of the railway on the space surrounding people and on their minds, the production processes of industrialisation were also an important background element for urban development in the previous century. Division of labour and the subdivision of previously integrated activities were clearly a basis for success in industrial production processes and were capable of producing radical transformations. Why then shouldn't the principles of industrial production be applied to communal life in the city?

When Henry Ford first perfected the division of labour in the construction of automobiles, architects and city planners were also inculcated with similar ideas: the city could be viewed as a functionally organised unit that divided labour and the house seen as a "machine for living". These ideas came to influence architects and city planners such as Le Corbusier in the 1920s, and these thoughts were an important background for the way in which street networks in the city and countryside were then developed.

Another new element also came to play a role around this time: In the 1890s and continuing in the period up to the beginning of the First World War, a widespread discussion and general support for an export-orientated economy began to predominate in the industrial states. The records of parliamentary debates from this period mirror the contemporary discussion of globalisation today. In the German Reichstag, more rights were already being demanded for automobile drivers before 1910 so that the German automobile industry would not suffer disadvantages in comparison to the automobile industry in the USA.[35] The relationship with distant locations and improved accessibility of new markets from one's own location became important factors that shaped the developing character of transport in industrialised states.

A discipline of transport history comparable to that of architectural history exists only in a fledgling form; several of these sources will be referred to in the following. The background, which will provide explanations from diverse sources regarding the development of transport in the cities and countryside, must still be elaborated in further research. This applies particularly to work in the field of "strollology", developed by Lucius Burckhardt, which deals with the changing view of the countryside from the vantage point of the railway, through postcards in the early period of mass tourism as well as the manner in which travel and trips were described. Cumulatively, a cultural and material context developed in the period of industrialisation that focused attention more on access to distant locations than on a relation to more proximate areas and destinations. Without an understanding of this background, the profound process of change in the nature of streets and the transport network that occurred in this period and the corresponding change in the urban experience cannot be fully appreciated.

The Separation of the House from the Street and the Loss of the Street as a Place to Spend Time

At the beginning of this book it was described how the street, the forecourt, and the house jointly form a unified entity that may then be used in a wide variety of ways. This is reflected in the forms the street takes, in social agreements about how the street is to be used, and in the language people employ. The idea of transferring the highly successful industrial approach to the division of labour onto the organisation of the city and the promotion and admiration of modern means of transportation that were oriented to long-distance connections quickly had a very concrete impact on this nexus of urban arrangements. This could be seen most immediately in the roadways passing through settlements. Step by step their highly diversified use, including even serving as a play area for children, was reduced to a single purpose: they became a vector for high-speed, motorised transport to distant locations.

This began around the beginning of the last century in a seemingly harmless fashion with the already mentioned automobile liability. This seemed an unimportant topic for the planning of urban localities but in fact it showed that a legal question can have a decisive impact on how urban space is configured.

Until approximately 1900, a more or less self-evident rule was in force: The operator of any particular technology in public places had to bear the risks associated with this technology and would be held liable in the event of damages. If persons were killed by the explosion of the first steam cars, if automobile drivers ran over chickens or dogs in the villages, then it was clear: the operator of the technology, the driver, had to pay if he didn't (as was frequently the case) simply flee the scene with his "high-speed" vehicle.

As the streets were very full of diverse forms of life at this time and automobiles were continually becoming larger and heavier, payment of damages soon became a very expensive proposition for motorists. Initial accounts in newspaper articles and books from the time reported mainly about single-car accidents affecting the driver through injury or death, but this soon changed with damages to third parties becoming ever more considerable. These damages began to assume dimensions that might have stopped the automobile in its development. The insurance policies for automobiles[36] developed in the course of industrialisation to cover large-scale technology were unaffordable even for the wealthiest drivers if drivers were to be made completely liable for all risks associated with their activity.

The Liability Act for Automobiles passed in 1909 (see Figures 3.6 and 3.7) in Germany still serves as an important basis for the law governing road transport. The new law specified that drivers were no longer responsible for all damages. Others could also be responsible for an accident, particularly if they were located on the roadway. This was the beginning of the end for the use of the roadway for pedestrians, playing children, and animals as a place that could be simply occupied.

Some elements of the old legal opinion that the street is to be understood as a public space serving all parties are still to be found in current law governing street

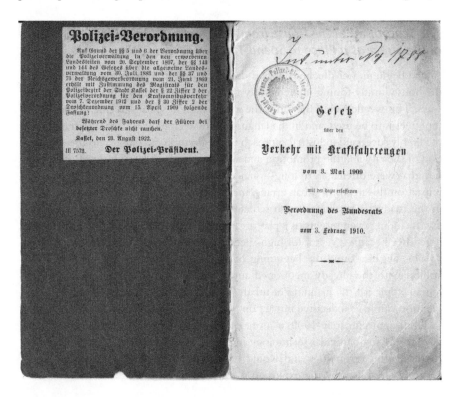

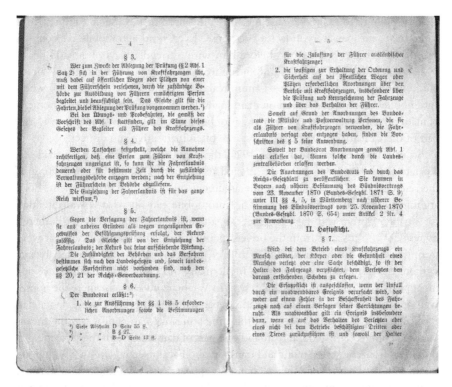

FIGURES 3.6 and 3.7   Excerpts from the "Act Regarding Transport with
Automobiles"—Germany's first road traffic code from 1909
(copy from the Kassel Police Department)

traffic in Germany, but these are of little real significance. There does exist a concept of "public use of the street" (everyone has a right to use the public streets), but this is severely limited by other laws and directives. In these provisions, the predominant right of the "flow of traffic" is defined. In practice, this means that a pedestrian may only cross the street when he takes the precedence of this flow into account. In today's traffic situation, this means that on extensive stretches of road there is no opportunity or only a very slight one to cross from one side of a street to the other—particularly on main thoroughfares.

In Germany the legal situation is such that in many cases (for example, if a crossover possibility is available within an "acceptable distance" through a traffic light or a pedestrian tunnel or bridge) contact with a "counterpart" on the other side of the street can only be achieved by means of an extensive detour.[37] Legal provisions thus have considerably altered the urban space in front of houses and buildings. The street that was once a space that facilitated a multitude of possibilities for the immediately adjacent persons has become a space of constant uncertainty and strain.

In this situation it is often overlooked that the material features and sheer weight of the automobile make the "equal use" of an area by automobiles and pedestrians or bicyclists simply infeasible.[38] While I can easily ask any person standing in my vicinity politely to make way for me, it is unrealistic to pose such a request to a parked car and expect a satisfactory response. Even if an automobile is occupied and the driver allows me to go before him with a friendly wave, I am still heavily dependent on him. Should his foot slip from the brake to the gas pedal—a rare but not unheard-of occurrence—I am in real danger. Still more dangerous is when automobiles drive at high speed on main roads; in this common situation a moment of inattentiveness can cost a pedestrian his or her life. Children, who make up a large part of the casualties in traffic accidents, are often inattentive and distracted.

So it is no wonder that by the 1920s the proposal had already been made to separate the house from the street. A kind of division of labour and protection of the residents from the traffic were the arguments made for this arrangement. Both arguments seemed to make sense. The automobile can do what it was intended for—namely, drive without disturbance—particularly well when it is not bothered by residents (so it seems from the driver's perspective). The houses, freed as it were from the street, can better fulfil their role of providing shelter for their inhabitants without the disturbance of the street. In Germany this resulted in the first development plans, particularly in Bauhaus designs in Weimar and Dessau, where the houses were turned away from the street. Paths, separated from the street, were designated for pedestrians. The traffic was until this time a means to an end; it was the means of connection to one's counterpart and one part of daily life. With the separation of the house from the street, traffic and transport also became an end in itself within the locality. In the Charter of Athens,[39] transport appears as its own function in the city, although it does not produce or reproduce. With the change in the understanding of space in the city, the space itself changes and the terms used to describe it.

Within this logic, the further consequences of dissolving the close relationship between the house and the street are disregarded. This dissolution is seen as a simplification and is also supported by an argument of greater safety. The people, so the argument goes, will be protected from the effects of automobile traffic, which is no longer directly before their doors.

The control over the street directly in front of the house granted to residents in social rules that developed over centuries was increasingly taken away from residents. City planning as a new discipline coming into existence in conjunction with industrialisation replaced the residents' own control with its specialised provisions. Just as the factory requires an engineer for the organisation of production, so the industrialised city needs a city planner.

The domination of the automobile on the roadways of the streets in various types of settlements has been a gradual process. At first, automobiles drove only rarely through many side streets and many smaller localities, and the vehicles were seen as a sort of novelty and attraction. On main streets and in large cities it soon became evident that the growing traffic required some regulating intervention. The first traffic lights in Europe were set up in the 1920s. In Germany a 3-metre-high traffic tower in Berlin is well known, which was imported in 1924 from New York. The individual attentiveness of persons was replaced by rules coming from without (this anyway was the impression of the time). Writers and other persons who were prominent in Germany at this time included the poet Kurt Tucholsky,[40] who commented on this development sceptically and negatively.

Not only did the streets change in this period but also the entire transport network. These changes have occurred in a long process that extends to the planning activities of today.

Changes in the Transport Networks

The form and differentiation of the network of streets and paths in settlements determine to an enormous degree the life that is led there and our overall impression of the urban environment. These ways are a sort of complement to the privately owned parcels of land, which the German author Dieter Hoffmann-Axthelm[41] points to for their decisive influence on urban connections. The various networks of ways through a settlement create the basis for our presence there, for the relationships between people, and for the production and consumption opportunities in the immediate vicinity.

At the beginning of the previous century these networks began to undergo the first changes in how they were used, followed by changes in the legal arrangements governing their use and later by alterations in their structural form. This affected the basic living conditions and possibilities very extensively, particularly when established connections and types of use were disturbed, interrupted, or could only be realised by resorting to various detours.

Initially this was a slow and very gradual process that seemingly had little effect. Motorised vehicles used the street networks in the settlements only sporadically. The first measures taken were not only in the interest of the motorists. Public authorities and offices at the same time pursued other purposes such as establishing more order and hygiene[42] in the densely populated cities. Animals (particularly pigs and chickens), which until this time (at least in the smaller cities in Europe) could roam freely, disappeared from the streets.[43] Children and youths, who with their ball-playing activities also put windowpanes at risk, could be forced from the streets step by step by invoking the imperatives of the automobile and directed to "designated" playgrounds or organised in sports clubs for more orderly instruction.

Initially, the relationship of the police and other authorities with motorised vehicles and their drivers was rather problematic. Drivers were often stopped or directed to drive at very low speeds. This, however, was not the case for long. The first motorist lobbying groups recognised how important a close cooperation with public authorities could be. They invited policemen to try driving motor vehicles themselves and developed close relationships with leading officials. Already prior to the First World War, children began receiving traffic safety instruction in school to ensure they respected the public spaces given over to the requirements of car drivers.[44] This initially had little effect on the communication networks of people in their localities. However, from today's perspective, we can see it as the first step leading to the present situation in which no child is allowed to play at the side of the street without "proper supervision".

Making the street free for the flow of motorised vehicles was only the first step. On this basis, motorists were provided with their own transport network free of charge—not the case incidentally with the establishment of the railway—even if it did need to be further developed. However, in this newly appropriated network, precisely the qualities and characteristics that had been typical of transport networks in settled areas in the past centuries (and have been described here in the previous chapters) were those factors that made for disturbances and difficulties from the standpoint of the new motorised users.

This applied most obviously to intersections—especially when they occurred at narrow intervals of less than 100 metres, which was often the case in city blocks built during the Gründerzeit period. At the intersections it was necessary for drivers to brake and reduce their speed as the intersecting street could harbour a significant risk for personal safety and the integrity of the vehicle—namely, another vehicle travelling on the perpendicular vector. In the early days, these might also be horse-drawn carriages or carts. At these multitudinous points of conflict (from the standpoint of the car drivers), collisions with fatalities soon began to occur, making it clear that a non-negotiable rule had to be observed: at intersections one had to drive carefully and slow down.

For the vehicles of that era, braking was exceedingly inconvenient. The automobiles were difficult to get into gear; it required great effort to operate the clutch and the gear stick. The brakes also needed greater force to be applied by the driver and far greater distance for the vehicle to come to a halt. And that was not all. If one had to turn at the intersection, the act of turning the steering wheel also required great effort. Even with very few automobiles on the streets in the city, the cumbersome and dangerous manoeuvres of braking and turning resulted very quickly in disturbances of one sort or another. Interactions between vehicle drivers or with other persons on the street did not make negotiating an intersection any simpler. From 1902 in Germany, drivers were required to make a hand signal when executing a turn.

By 1907, official traffic signs were already being put up in Germany to better discipline the persons on the road.[45] That these first traffic signs were installed by the automobile lobby (i.e. the first automobile clubs) is indicative of the fact that this sort of regulation was in their interest.[46] Indeed these signs, in addition to alerting drivers about risks such as bumps in the road, were used almost everywhere in Europe to ban pedestrians from the roadway. The problematic issues referred to in the signs were from the standpoint of the automobiles and their occupants. In 1908 the international street congresses of the AIPCR (World Road Association) commenced (the first meeting in Paris had 2,411 participants from 33 different countries). In 1910 four internationally used warning signs for motorists were agreed upon. Warnings were designed for ruts, curves, intersections, and railway crossings. At the same time, it was decided how streets should look. They should be as straight as possible, appropriately wide, and not too steep, with curves that could be negotiated without significant reductions in speed.

In retrospect it is truly remarkable with what energy and intent a strategy for introducing and supporting the automobile was put into effect by the leading bourgeois, industrial, and administrative elements of society.

As a first step in Germany, the limitation of strict liability for the automobile was achieved without making driving too expensive (in the year 1910).[47] Similar success was achieved in the very swift acquisition of control over the transport networks in the settlements. Throughout this process there was a broad, internationally consistent argumentation that was used to implement these measures. Whatever could not be achieved on a local or national level was decided in international conferences (typically without democratic authorisation) and then put into effect, making reference to these conferences. One example of this was the street congresses conducted by AIPCR[48] that brought together "specialists" who then realised the decided policy on the national and local level, referring to the agreements that had been made at the congresses.

Within the various localities there were now significant obstacles in realising the principles described above—such as the demand for straight streets without intersections or such "bothersome" road users as pedestrians. At the periphery of the localities there were fewer problems. In Berlin, for example, construction had already begun in 1913 on a straight motorway exclusively for the use of cars, which later became the race track AVUS.[49] Model projects such as this increased the pressure to modify the existing street network as much as possible to conform to these standards.

The demands of motorists to be provided with streets that allowed fast driving unimpeded by intersections were met only bit by bit within localities, but nonetheless their wishes had clear and extensive effects very quickly. In Germany the first traffic signs for pedestrians were put up in 1905 to prohibit them from crossing certain streets. In 1917 in Berlin there was a traffic ordinance that stipulated the perpendicular crossing of any roadway by pedestrians.[50] At this time there were approximately 700 inhabitants in Berlin for each automobile. In effect, 699 persons had to change their behaviour so that one person could drive with more convenience.

In the 1920s, the idea of a "right of way" began to mark the end of car drivers having to stop at each intersection. Traffic on main roads was given right of way at intersections (in Germany these main roads were the so-called "Landesstrassen" (state roads) of the first order and later also "Reichsstrassen"). Traffic on the perpendicular thoroughfares had to yield. This principle corresponded exactly with the ideas of the engineers who sought to build the first intersection-free highways in Germany, Italy, and France. The model here was again the above-mentioned AVUS highway in Berlin (which at that time was classified as a test road and not a "true" highway).[51]

In 1929 the German "Studiengesellschaft für Automobilstraßenbau (STUFA)" (Research Institute for the Construction of Automobile Roadways) published preliminary guidelines for city streets. The basis of the approach presented in the guidelines was to create a master framework of main streets in the cities that should have the characteristic of allowing "non-stop traffic as much as possible". To put it differently, the city was to be traversed with streets that were orientated to long-distance travel; local transport and above all the pedestrians living and working in the city would have to yield to these new streams of traffic.

The guidelines also described how these streets should have the function of lowering the amount of traffic on other thoroughfares. This laid the foundation for a basic error in transport planning that continues today. The belief is that planning and street construction using "street widening"—particularly the construction of so-called bypass roads and other traffic-channelling measures—can reduce the amount of traffic in the city centre or other specific parts of the city. This has been promulgated in Germany by the STUFA since 1929 and continues to be the basis for many transport construction projects. In fact, however, the real effect of these various bypass measures is to increase the transport surface area devoted to automobiles. Furthermore, the general practice of granting the high-speed, long-distance automobile traffic on such bypass streets right of way has the effect of forcing local traffic to yield and wait and be blocked by this other type of traffic flow.

Whether these bypass streets (also known as beltways or ring roads) disturb pedestrian or bicyclist access to the surrounding countryside or whether they separate parts of the city as main transport axes, the end effect is that local connections are systematically degraded and long-distance connections based on automobile transport are improved. In this way, very early in the history of the automobile an enormous and disproportionate redistribution of space for the use of cars was achieved. This end was reached mainly through the use of judicial and administrative measures. The construction of new streets was presented as part of a new and highly desirable model; it seemed to make an emerging utopia visible. This process could be described economically as follows: A basic reorganisation or priorities took place. Massive investments were made in long-distance automobile-based transport and this was accompanied by a significant disinvestment in a variety of local, non-automobile-based networks.

This development did not at all correspond with the predominant demand of the times. Automobile ownership in Germany rose in the final years of the 1920s from approximately one vehicle per 100 persons to one vehicle per fifty persons at the beginning of the 1930s, although the majority of these vehicles were motorcycles.[52] On the other hand, the need for space to accommodate everyday non-automobile-based mobility and diverse types of communication and activity in the areas in front of and around urban dwellings grew significantly as a result of ongoing population growth. The architectural and urban development visions of those years (one of many examples is that of Le Corbusier with his "Plan Voisin" for Paris of 1925[53]) featured huge provisions for automobile traffic.

The predominance of such views did not come from the general population but rather from a much more particular segment of the society. The automobile corresponded completely with the technology-dominated interests and future visions of the leading intellectual, financial, and political classes. The success of modern technologies—the bigger the better, whether in the form of ships or factories or skyscrapers—convinced these decision makers of the necessity and benefits of taking an essentially technical, technology-based approach to the question of urban settlement and living arrangements. The technicians themselves, usually architects or street planners (the first urban planners), saw their influence grow the more they made use of industrial principles, methods, and facilities in the cities. The new provisions for the automobile were a very important element in this process. The everyday, small-scale relationships between the house and the street, and the social implications of these connections that have been examined in previous chapters of this book, were not accorded the same degree of attention and were given a much lower priority, if any.

This is not a "natural" or inevitable development. Architects and urban planners also have an everyday life as ordinary people. A kind of split[54] between the human and social reality took place with the effect that the planning process itself became asocial. People are not viewed as complete, multi-faceted individuals, but rather as purpose-driven units. An individual standing at the entrance to his house who waves to a neighbour, checks that all is well with a group of children who are playing on the street, and then walks to the next corner mixes leisure, shopping, and child-rearing activities in one integrated series of actions. This behaviour was now handled as a set of discrete social functions, supposedly allowing for greater efficiency but in fact ignoring the complex multi-layered local processes that make up urban life.

The "pedestrian", to the extent that he was taken into account at all, was viewed simply as a means of transport, not as a person present in an urban space. The planners created a corresponding hierarchy in their networks: residential streets, collecting roads, transit roads, main roads, and highways. In Germany, the most important streets are those of the "first order"; the others belong to a subordinate network. In this terminology the functional separation in the network corresponds to the functional separation in the city. In the technical hierarchy the determining role that streets have was made clear to all concerned. The important streets are "preferred". These are the streets that lead to distant places, the ones on which the cars can drive faster and that are particularly wide and well constructed.

A transformation occurred. The original type of city, in which local relationships and activities in the direct vicinity of the house defined everyday life, where the interests of the local residents and those of persons passing through were brought into agreement on a piecemeal basis at the various intersections, was transformed into a city where long-distance concerns and automobile transport were the dominant forces. To some extent the utopian-minded planners of the 1920s seemed to be aware of the disadvantages coming from these developments. They laid out the through roads as arterial routes to avoid disturbing the everyday life and local forms of urban communication, and even considered having the automobiles pass through the cities in tunnels.

This was in some instances possible by making use of subways and urban rail lines, which could transport a large volume of people with a narrowly constructed transport vector. Such forms of transport could be arranged in a manner that did not excessively disturb existing urban situations. The routes required for cars, on the other hand, were so wide, and the expense and effort to realise such plans so large, that it was impossible to finance such construction plans, although their formulation is another demonstration of just how important long-distance connections were deemed to be by the urban planners of that era. Today we know, in addition, that elevated roadways or tunnels for automobile traffic can only be realised with an enormous sacrifice of urban space as well as other liabilities.

As soon as the new transport networks for cars were realised, they began to have the effect of confirming the assumptions of their planners. They were quite quickly filled with automobiles. To be sure, many years passed before traffic congestion began to occur outside of urban localities. But within the cities, even small numbers of automobiles managed to create traffic chaos at important points. While a pedestrian requires only a small amount of space and can adapt flexibly to changing conditions, each automobile requires a significantly larger amount of space which becomes even greater as the cars travel faster.

Because of these characteristics, their size, and the noise they produced, the initially small numbers of cars drew more attention in the urban context than the children who could no longer play in the front yard of houses located in the city. All attention was directed to the automobile. The planners and architects, who at the time were drawing their visions of future cities, were themselves typically car drivers and saw the city from the vantage point of the automobile. This view was directed principally at obstacles that could impede free forward travel for the automobile and at what they saw as risks – curves, intersections, crossing traffic, whether pedestrians or other vehicles. The demand for "more space" was confirmed from a specious perspective advocating the requirements of the automobile, with a degree of influence that should not be underestimated.

It was thus physical changes in the urban landscape and a resulting spatial experience that allowed the automobile to advance as a defining element of the urban experience. Nearly all of the works dealing with the history of the automobile neglect this aspect and the losses and disadvantages imposed through the redistribution of space in the cities. The persons directly affected in the various localities did not in the least greet these developments with the same cheers heard as vehicles passed by at the first race tracks.

These losses were by no means accepted without opposition by the persons affected,[55] but the history of such protests is nearly forgotten today. The protests had some success, albeit mostly outside of the cities. In the canton Graubünden in Switzerland, for instance, there was a general ban on automobile traffic from 1900 to 1925 that was regularly confirmed by popular referendums. Such actions, however, did not affect the general and accumulating loss of the street as a free space available to a multitude of different parties and its transformation into an automobile-dominated vector breaking up the urban landscape.[56]

The solution offered by the specialists to the general public is to be found in the architectural visions developed as the automobile gained in predominance: a new "quiet" form of urban living that is turned away from the street. Already in the mid-1920s, the first ribbon developments were constructed where houses were not orientated to the structures on the other side of the street but looked out to the back. There were no longer streets between these structures. The argument made for such an approach was based on social considerations supposedly in the interests of the residents joined to the increasingly predominant outlook of a particular bourgeois lifestyle that associated nature and sunlight with good health. With structures that stood one behind the other backed off from the street, the connections from house to house were broken. As the length of the houses increased, access to a fictive "neighbour across the way" could only be gained in a very roundabout manner.

As set down in the "Charter of Athens", streets were no longer to be combined with footways and local communication.[57] This of course was contrary to the communicative function that the street had fulfilled over thousands of years. The "Charter of Athens", heavily influenced by Le Corbusier, separates automobile traffic in accordance with the basic idea of a functionally defined urban entity in which various types of transport are each handled separately and distinctly. The "protection" of the residents against various traffic by-products such as noise is emphasised in this document. In fact, however, the spatial separation of transport from other urban functions can also be viewed as the diversion of all these other functions into reservations between the streets intended for automobile traffic. Viewed from this perspective, the "protection" can also be seen as an excuse for allowing the automobile to drive without any obstacles or disturbances at maximum speed.[58]

A perusal of the "Charter of Athens" is often an occasion for surprise for contemporary planners who still advocate the shifting of automobile traffic and then judge the Charter to be a work that "looked far into the future",[59] or that cleverly anticipated today's traffic-management measures. This shows more than anything that the often expressed opinion that criticism of the "Charter of Athens" today is superfluous and no longer relevant is incorrect. In fact, many of the basic principles from the Charter have shaped the assumptions of contemporary urban planning and zoning law, and many of the purportedly "alternative" plans are more similar to the erroneous principles of the Charter than their authors imagine. This also applies to the principle of functional separation in the city,[60] which is far better known than the statements regarding transport. Today it is in any case clear that a city that truly features small-scale, mixed-use planning in fact produces far less automobile traffic than cities relying on purely residential areas.[61] The functional separation itself gives rise to a substantial segment of the automobile traffic, which it then shifts to another location.

How much sense does it really make to endeavour to direct automobile traffic around residential areas? To begin with, this assumes that people do not live everywhere in the city and particularly not on the main streets. Until the present day, however, it has not been possible to realise the demand of fully functional separation in the European city. Studies show that even in industrial areas a surprisingly high number of regular residents are to be found and that this is actually not so bad. Simply for reasons of security, it is important to have some persons present even in functionally separated structures. Persons live along many main streets and even along urban motorways.

Even if it should be possible to "isolate" the main thoroughfares from regular residences—as planners dreamed in the "Charter of Athens" at the beginning of the 1930s—the traffic must still drive to and from these main thoroughfares. Up to the present day it can be observed that when traffic is shifted (onto urban motorways for instance), the volume of traffic travelling parallel to the new bypass roadways may decrease, but the volume of traffic on the exit and entry streets (the perpendicularly orientated routes) continues to increase. Creation of such new roadways in any case creates a larger surface area for automobile transport within the city and on a long-term basis stimulates growth in vehicular transport. As already mentioned, the end result of this "strategy" of shifting traffic since its commencement in the 1920s is that there are only a very limited number of streets where a long-term decline in automobile traffic can be demonstrated.

At a tactical level, this strategy of shifting the traffic flow—and the accompanying hierarchisation and extension of the street network—represented a highly intelligent model for success. The people agreed to new streets when they were promised that this would relieve traffic congestion, and these promises were (and continue to be) believed by those who see no other way of avoiding the ever-increasing burdens created by automobiles in the city. This same reasoning continues to be used today when new street construction is discussed, and often enough it is successful.

The basis for this argumentation is also to be found in the "Charter of Athens", significantly shaped by the influence of Le Corbusier. The Charter includes a section devoted to traffic and transport in the form of fourteen theses and accompanying explanations. Here, for example, the illusion can be found (Thesis 63) that everything in the urban realm—from taking walks to high-speed car travel—would be better if a "fundamental reform of transport" were to occur. The long-distance streets "will have no occasion to have public or private structures in their vicinity"; they should disappear behind "thick green hedges". One should have known that this could not occur without drawbacks, as the same Charter criticises the separation of urban districts by railroad lines (Thesis 58). If a rail line has the deleterious effect of breaking up urban neighbourhoods, then what will be the effect of the many new long-distance streets hidden behind their green hedges?

In the "Charter of Athens", a vision of the future is formulated from the perspective of the car drivers. A chief obstacle appearing in the middle of this argumentation is a feature of the street that has made life difficult for car drivers from the beginning, namely the intersection. The first section devoted to transport in the Charter (Thesis 51) identifies the street network of the city as the "sum of branches". Thesis 54 then lets it be known: "The distances between the street intersections is too small." The reason for this is purely technical: "The brakes cannot be used so intensively without causing a very rapid deterioration of important components." The braking system of the automobile thereby provides a key argument for the complete transformation of the urban street network. The fact that the small-scale local communication networks in the cities had previously served the communication needs of the populace does not receive any attention here.

We have already made reference to the multitude of possibilities provided by small-scale transport networks that had developed slowly over time in various urban settings. It is now necessary to supplement this depiction with findings from modern communication studies. The works of Vilém Flusser[62] on communication networks and the capabilities he ascribes to small-scale communication in open networks (so-called network dialogues) are clear. He characterises such dialogues—one basis for which is an adequate everyday street network in cities and towns—as "the foundation of all communication and thus the human engagement against death". Changes in urban communication networks are thus not just relevant for the condition of automobile brake shoes.

The rise of the automobile not only led to the loss of the street as a place and a resource for the people, it also resulted in an entirely new network configuration in existing settlements. The long-distance orientation of such networks and their concentration on long-distance transport were apparent to anyone who made use of them, particularly in the cities. This was not only the case for Germany. The transformation of these networks was an important point of orientation for all persons. Local needs and the qualities operative in the immediate environment had to take second place to long-distance domination. Rapid communication predominated over slower everyday forms of communication. This circumstance, which could be perceived daily for many in their normal affairs, had significant effects, one of these being to increase the attractiveness of the automobile. Everyone could see that the car owner and the person coming from a distance were deemed to be of greater importance by urban planners and the leading figures of the cities, and that these parties would be promoted. The use of space communicated a message that was very clear. Distance was preferred over proximity. Those who let themselves be orientated to the immediate environment were less advanced. What is happening in Rome or New York is what counts; what is occurring with my neighbour or in my immediate vicinity is of less significance.

The mindset that assigned great and decisive significance for peripheral realms to distant, global events was enormously reinforced in the period of the 1930s and during the ensuing World War. Whether it was a global economic crisis occurring as a consequence of a stock market crash in New York that resulted in the dismissal of a worker in a provincial German city or the war itself that brought reports from distant locales that included information about death and injury to family members, people came to be affected by distant developments in very direct ways in their local settings.

Indeed, sometimes it was even necessary to flee to distant points to save oneself—from German fascism, for example. The war and the preparations for war emphasised the critical role of technology and planning in Germany. The transport networks (initially primarily the railways), logistic systems, spare parts for vehicles and the reliability of the vehicles themselves—all this was decisive in the military slaughter that would ensue in the aggressive war the fascists were already preparing. The initial victory of National Socialist Germany and its allies demonstrated once again the strength that derives from being able to move men and materials quickly using modern means of transport.

Germany more than any other state displayed enormous expertise in planning—not only in the area of war preparations, but also in everything from creating transport facilities to possessing an exact picture of the transport facilities in the localities of the conquered territories (this all connected with the destruction of "unfitting" places and the murder of "unfitting" persons). The authors Gert Gröning and Joachim Wolschke-Bulmahn in their 1987 work[63] already showed how the development of landscape management and land-use planning in Germany after the Second World War was inextricably connected with the SS leader and mass murderer Heinrich Himmler, and the planning staff used to coordinate the "push to the East". Other information that later came to light indicates that the connections of many planners to the Nazi Party were even closer than these authors could show in their groundbreaking work.[64]

In nearly all of the development planning, whether in Germany for the construction of new cities, in conquered areas or for the renovation of existing urban centres, the National Socialist functionaries stepped away from classic permeable street grids with many intersections at short intervals. This is particularly evident in the work of a planner and architect who played an important role in the reconstruction and transformation of the street network in the Federal Republic of Germany after the war—Hans Bernhard Reichow.

Hans Bernhard Reichow became the head of municipal planning in Braunschweig in 1934. He moved into planning administration in Stettin in 1936 and became director of building there in 1939. Reichow developed a residential model for the city and surrounding area that is broken into settlement units. With the so-called "West-Oder" route, a linear settlement, his residential model received an access infrastructure that was suited to automobile traffic with fast, well-constructed streets. The settlement units were orientated to this access route like the local groups of the Nazi Party NSDAP to the guidelines of the central party organisation—as Reichow chose to picture it.[65] The entire system was constructed in accordance with a strict hierarchy.

Hans Bernhard Reichow joined the NSDAP in 1937. As in similar cases, this is often judged to have been "necessary for his career". Actually (it is purported), he had his differences with the National Socialists. Clear proof for this or for another view is not conclusively available, but the excellent work of Katja Bernhardt opens the door to other interpretations.[66] Reichow described himself in retrospect as "too modern". Expressly in the 1940s, the technological/modernising wing of the NSDAP under Albert Speer was setting the tone, and Reichow belonged to the party's "Task Force for the Reconstruction of Destroyed Cities". In his de-nazification proceedings his membership in the Nazi SA was also apparently established. He was able to get through the proceedings without formal charges with the assistance of various character witnesses.

In the years directly following the war, Reichow became one of the most publicly effective planners in the reconstructive efforts in cities in the new Federal
Republic. He took his old designs from the war years and declared them to be
new. What shortly before was understood to be a city plan based on the model of
the National Socialist party, he now called an "organic"[67] form and later an "automobile-orientated"[68] design, although the form and ordering principles remained
essentially unchanged. After the war, the same hierarchical tree structure of the
communication network was said to be similar to that found in leaves or in the
blood circulation of the lungs (see Figure 3.8).

The networks designed by Reichow were not grid patterns and they did not
include main roads or priority streets with right of way. In his designs, the phenomenon of the intersection (the car drivers' difficult moment) had disappeared
completely. In the tradition of the Charter of Athens, he proposed a separation
of all different types of transport: foot and bicycle paths would be separated from
roads for cars. In this model, the footpaths did not form a network but were rather
integrated in the tree structure.[69]

The influence of Reichow's work, which was promoted in the newly created
Federal Republic of Germany and disseminated in training films, is often underestimated by specialists in the field. In fact, Reichow's influence was enormous,

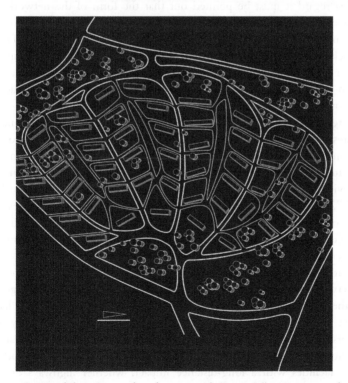

FIGURE 3.8   Automobile-orientated settlement with "organic" access network
(drawing: Jan Houdek, freely adapted from Hans Bernhard Reichow)

particularly as regards the constitutive image of the city. His identification of cities with the human body, the view of traffic as the "blood circulation" and the comparison of the transport infrastructure with the vascular system of a tree: these ways of thinking found a place in everyday speech and not just in Germany. The arterial road that is clogged or congested, the "Verkehrsinfarkt" (traffic infarction or congestion) on the model of the coronary infarction which would bring the entire city to the point of death – these are images that go back to Reichow and his pictorial analogies.

Even more important for the success of similar approaches in countries around the world were the clear hierarchies and ordering systems included in Reichow's approach. Long-distance connections, which were so important in the course of the war and which seemed to be becoming even more important in post-war society with a system depending on worldwide exchange, dominated Reichow's plans. Local connections had to take a subordinate position. Continuous, small-scale networks for pedestrians hardly existed in his plans; their paths were of secondary importance and were orientated merely to the next bus stop at the next main street. Investments were made in creating major connections for automobiles. Small-scale communication was banished to places specially reserved for such activities, but at which there was no real occasion for communication.

In this regard it must be pointed out that the form of the networks (as we know not only from the works of Vilém Flusser) are of decisive importance in determining how communication actually happens in everyday life. The forms that Reichow developed are remarkably similar to his plans for organising space in accordance with the model of the local party units of the NSDAP. The aim was clearly to establish dominance over dispersed localities through large-scale control mechanisms.

As a result of the removal of intersections in the access-providing networks, the routes are predetermined; there are no accidental meetings. The continuous "flow" and the frictionless character of the motion ensure that human contacts only occur if planned—and thus almost never arise in the incidental manner necessary for vital urban living. In addition, it is simple to control a given district from "outside". Whoever has control of the access point can take note of everything entering or leaving the district and restrict that traffic as desired. The similarity of the form of transport access with the organisation of a fascistic party is not entirely without consequences.[70]

Similar forms need not always have similar causes. However, the fact that in other networks of exchange (for example, in the modern transport of goods and cargo) the forms with similarities to Reichow's network organisation have also prevailed should give us pause. It is indisputable that in contemporary societies those persons who travel far, fast and wide have a pronounced dominance over those who are confined to a local or regional context. Likewise, even today those transport facilities with a long-distance impact, whether highways or airports, receive far more attention in the associated organisational and planning activities than small-scale communication on streets or urban squares.

The Prevalence of Distance-Orientated Planning in the 1950s and 60s, and the Isolation of Residents in New Fordist Forms of Settlement

The decision to orient forms of settlement towards long-distance factors was not an "automatic" development or one that planners were forced to make in response to the general public's "free choice for the automobile". No—the planning and construction of new forms of organising space in residential settlements came far in advance of any actual decisions made by the persons involved. The new forms of settlement are well described by the word "Fordist"—which only later came to have a role in the discipline of sociology. Clear and definite allocation of roles and "lines of command" also shaped the production organisation in the early stages of capitalism.

The basic forms of cities in Europe in their structural form remained orientated to small-scale communication at the end of the Second World War, even if newly established traffic rules, street ordinances and street construction had already begun to give the automobile far more rights than were consistent with its actual significance. Preparation was thus being made for the future urban forms in the traditional network. An opportunity to make radical changes in the structural form of the urban infrastructure through the demolition of existing buildings and the redevelopment of streets came at the end of the war. Many cities had suffered severe damage in the course of the conflict. In addition, the idea arose that a "new beginning" was called for, which should also take shape in a transformed urban infrastructure.

In Germany, the clearing away of debris and destruction caused in the war was often combined with false (as we shall later see) propaganda regarding a new beginning. In the city of Kassel, for example, where aerial bombing by British and American forces had substantially destroyed the city centre on 22 to 23 October 1943, the post-war planners did everything they could to have even more buildings condemned that were not already destroyed, particularly when such structures blocked new plans for street construction. At the same time, an exhibition was opened with great ceremony under the title "Kassel Rebuilds". The distortions and at times outright lies that were used in this connection were eventually discovered.[71] It became clear that the extent of the destruction had been exaggerated at those points where buildings stood in the way of the new layout for the city so as to be able to tear down "inconvenient structures".

The idea of a "new beginning" also was discredited, and in such a way that it was necessary for the planners to close down their exhibition. The plans that were presented at the exhibition turned out in large part to be identical to the visions of a fascist "Gau-Hauptstadt Kassel"[72] produced by Nazi planners before the destruction of the city. Apparently, leading planners from Albert Speer's "Task Force for the Reconstruction of Destroyed Cities" such as Konstanty Gutschow and Hans Bernhard Reichow were involved in the effort. In this instance, as in many others in post-war Germany,[73] the people doing the work were the same as those who had been responsible for planning in the National Socialist urban administration activities.[74]

After the public reaction prevented direct realisation of the old Nazi plans in post-war Kassel, a competition of well-known engineers was held to provide the city with a new layout. After a fair amount of back and forth, a plan emerged that, while not entirely similar to the old fascist plans, had many of its main elements in a lightly disguised form, and when realised had the effect of fully transforming the historical urban layout and infrastructure of the city.

The main components of these changes have already been described in the previous chapters. A great number of intersections disappeared and the entire network became in effect more widely meshed. In those places where the old street layout was followed, the old intersecting streets were simply cut off (see Figure 3.9).

For example, on a wide, axis-like main street, the side street has been made into a dead end. That this side street in earlier times continued over the main street can be seen in the identical name of the truncated street on both sides of the "through way" that has thus been created. This street has now become a sort of inner-city autobahn that has no intrinsic relationship to the buildings that surround it. The former urban street has become simply a place to pass through.

The ideas that Le Corbusier had formulated demanding an urban landscape with long straight streets on which one needn't brake when driving came to be realised increasingly in the emerging form of street networks put into place after the war. Of course, this changed the character of these networks not only for automobiles

FIGURE 3.9 The Kölnische Strasse in Kassel: After the completion of the inner-city ring, the previously continuous street near the Scheidemannplatz was cut off and made into a dead end (photograph: Swen Schneider)

but also for pedestrians and bicyclists. It also caused a radical change in the relationship of residential structures to the street. In places where such buildings were newly constructed after the war to alleviate the shortage of living space, they were built in long rows that were orientated perpendicularly to the street. On the streets themselves, the automobile soon came to dominate in a more imposing fashion than before the war.

In 1953 in Germany all existing speed limits for automobiles were abolished—also within city and village limits. The fascist administration, as previous chapters have made clear, was always an advocate of unrestricted automobile use. However, in 1939 it was necessary to introduce speed limits partly because of a general fuel shortage as the war effort grew and also because of the growing use of Buna artificial rubber tyres, which were produced owing to shortages in the supply of natural rubber. These tyres could only withstand driving at reduced speeds. Therefore, in 1939, purely because of these restraints, a speed limit of 100 km per hour for cars and 70 km per hour for trucks outside of localities and a speed limit between 40 and 60 km per hour inside localities were implemented. In 1953, all of these limits were abolished, partly with the argument that this represented the elimination of a "Nazi law". The relatively small number of automobiles on the roads in the immediate post-war years nonetheless created a substantial risk. Only after four years and many fatalities on the streets in the cities and villages was a general speed limit of 50 km per hour introduced in 1957 in Germany for automobiles within localities.[75]

The risks created by automobiles became an important basis for giving the automobile further privileges. It was deemed inappropriate for pedestrians and bicyclists to make use of higher-speed streets; when required, they were forced to follow detours and to make use of tunnels or bridges to reach their destinations. This was a central precept of Hans Bernhard Reichow. With his treatise on the "automobile-orientated city", which was distributed by the responsible building administration as a semi-official guideline, Reichow became the institutionally supported theoretician of this new form of urban planning.[76]

Although much of what Reichow presented simply seems peculiar (his equation of the city with leaves, trees or the human blood circulation system, for instance), one should not underestimate his influence. He made films about his theories that were widely distributed and also shown to children in schools, presenting the view that the city should not be based on an open grid layout as had been the case for thousands of years, but rather should have a hierarchical form going from main transport streets to a system of smaller branches ending ultimately in dead ends.

The concept of the tree structure for new urban districts was accepted in almost all of Europe, and it is no accident that it corresponds with the hierarchical processes that predominated in business entities at that time. The 1965 work of the urban planner Christopher Alexander titled *A City is Not a Tree*[77] attempted in an almost despairing fashion to protest against these developments and their continuing realisation. Today in Germany and elsewhere in Europe, one can typically determine whether the street layout of a given urban district was set up before the 1950s or after.

Hierarchical street networks do not come into existence by themselves. Important elements of a particular belief in the future typical of the mid-twentieth century are reflected in the concept of order they embody. Not only the long, straight streets as a symbol of the orientation of any particular settlement to distant locations and the triumph of speed over space, but also the step-by-step gradation from top to bottom (corresponding to workplace hierarchies) culminating in the lowest (and least significant) street in the immediate vicinity of a personal residence make it clear that this is a physical manifestation of a belief in technological progress and the hierarchical division of labour in industrial production. The shifting of the orientation of houses away from the street is another formal rule that emerges in this urban form.

The construction of houses in rows came to dominate in new post-war planning. On leaving their homes, people no longer looked at the front of the house across the street but at the back of another house. The impression of the isolation and separation of residences without a connection by means of the street to a larger urban entity is particularly evident in single-family housing tracts[78]—a state of isolation that corresponds with the situation of the industrial worker at the conveyor belt. The principle of an industrial division of labour also came to be a model for the flow of traffic. The "separation" of types of transport, and thus the "optimisation" of pedestrian and bicycle paths that were removed from the streets reserved for the automobile, was seen as the goal. What was lost as a vision (and as a reality) was the fact that the unity of house, street, sidewalk and other structures makes sense for the people living in such settings. A pedestrian path that goes through a tunnel, for example, loses the security in night-time use that comes from potential contact with drivers on a shared street.

Of course, it was not only Reichow's propagandistically employed analogy of the city to the human body or to trees that opened the way to a concept of a hierarchically organised, long-distance-orientated urban transport infrastructures and layouts. In the USA, a very similar, even more distance-orientated form of urban organisation developed corresponding to the prevailing conditions of modern capitalism found there. This happened relatively independently from the developments in Germany and Europe with an even stronger emphasis on the participation of industrial interests.

In his work *The Option of Urbanism*, Christopher B. Leinberger describes in an impressive fashion how in the summer months of 1939 and 1940 a World's Fair held in New York presented a vision of the world of tomorrow to the people in the form of a "Futurama". The background for the presentation of this vision of the future was prepared and influenced by the leading representatives of modernism, such as Le Corbusier, Walter Gropius, Mies van der Rohe, and Ludwig Hilberseimer.[79] The major sponsor of the exhibition was General Motors.[80] The city of tomorrow was shown in the form of giant panoramas, high-altitude perspectives, and a street intersection in 1:1 format. Separation of different forms of traffic, an urban layout using central "traffic arteries", and a hinterland filled with singly standing one-family houses were presented to the astonished visitors with a level of media resources that was unprecedented for the time. At its conclusion, the exhibition had hosted 55 million visitors.

Through these visitor numbers and extensive media coverage, the vision of the future presented there remained a force in US society over several years, influencing campaign platforms and the dominant ideas about the future among politicians and taking form in a complex web of political and business interests. The investments over the succeeding decades in the realisation of the image of the future presented there—that of a large-scale street and road network erected by the state—generated one of the largest power centres in America next to the military complex. Leinberger describes how billions of dollars were invested in this new image of the landscape of tomorrow. An interwoven system of business and state interests grew up that advocated and realised a continuous extension of this network as well as its ongoing maintenance.

Thus it was not only in Germany or in Europe that a form of development was introduced that was orientated to distant points. The transfer of the logic of an industrially based division of labour onto the question of how to organise urban space was also propagated in the USA as a self-evident proposition. Active here were not only various industrial interests but also a growing state power block located in governmental departments having to do with construction, transport and commerce, as well as such dedicated power centres as the US Federal Highway Administration. It was not only the logic of fascism that promoted the push towards distant points; the logic of the industrial system as such also promoted such an orientation very strongly. The connection of investments in transport with such core concepts of capitalism as "growth" and "prosperity" propelled it still further. At the same time, the rise of the engineer as a figure and a profession shaping people's everyday lives continued, as did the concomitant rise of the automobile—twin phenomena that proceeded in the main without any democratic checks or controls.

This can be seen again in the example of Germany, where in the 1950s and 60s so-called "general transport plans" were enacted, featuring immense and unprecedented interventions to promote and facilitate the use of automobiles in the cities.

The Development of the Street Network

In the cities of Germany, it was only possible to realise the post-war plans for development of the street network if substantial parts of the existing urban layout were subjected to at times massive changes—in the existing buildings and in privately held property lots. The bombing damage suffered in the Second World War was in many instances merely a pretext for realising such changes, as has already been shown in the example of Kassel. Often, however, this pretext alone was not sufficient to overcome the resistance of the local inhabitants to these transformative plans. Preparation for the automobile-orientated future was not only promoted with the training films of the urban planner Reichow, but also through the activities of numerous engineers and technicians in the form of mathematically derived prognosis models of some future reality, which were invoked to argue the inherent necessity of a particular set of planning decisions. Such prognosis models were originally developed in the USA to show the expected traffic and transport volume associated with future land use and were adopted by German transport engineers and used in German cities in a slightly modified form.

The equation systems used in these prognosis models—which generally only addressed automobile traffic—were in fact quite simple. On the basis of statistical analyses (multiple regression) that rarely went beyond positing linear connections between the volume of automobile traffic on the streets and the population development (often combined with factors such as income or automobile ownership), traffic volume in the past was determined and projected into imaginary or concretely planned future circumstances.

Over time, these prognosis models came to be used in a four-step process. In the first step, the existing traffic volume in a given study area is determined. This area (called a transport cell) is typically a relatively self-contained area with a radius of several hundred meters or more depending on the degree of exactitude. Then divisions are made between the different types of transport in use (in those infrequent instances when another means of transport besides the automobile is considered).[81] In a third step, the traffic between the individual "cells" is calculated, whereby some models make use of an analogy to Newton's gravitational theory for their calculations. In a final step, the calculated traffic volumes between the "transport cells" are divided among existing or planned streets (referred to as the "route split"). The results of such models are then impressively presented as a bar chart showing "traffic load" (see Figure 3.10).[82]

Generally the transport engineers of the 1950s and 60s in Germany were trained civil engineers who during the war years had acquired professional

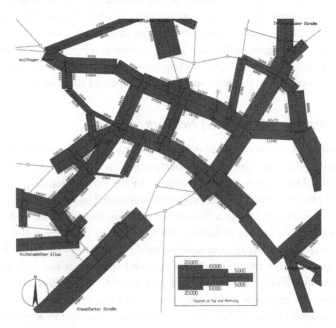

FIGURE 3.10 Bar chart from a general transport plan for the city of Kassel, Germany
(diagram: City of Kassel 1988; graphic rendering: Swen Schneider)

experience in logistics or in the design and construction of bunkers or other wartime constructions. This was also the case in other countries in this period. For example, Sir Colin Buchanan, who had a formative planning role in Great Britain (and beyond) in the 1960s, served as a combat engineer in the British Army during the war. In Germany, however, many of these planners had been closely associated with fascist organisations (for example, "Organisation Todt"). The Stuttgart professor Kurt Leibbrand was one of the most influential German transport engineers after the Second World War. He ultimately faced prosecution for war crimes in the 1960s.[83]

All transport planners of this period shared an orientation to a style of thinking and analysis that comes from static engineering, an area in which most of them had had experience during the war. In static engineering, a given "load" must be carried by a sufficiently sized beam in a house or girder in the roof of a bunker to ensure it can bear this weight; otherwise the structure will collapse. Transferred to the field of transport, this meant that a given traffic "load"—indicated on the typically used bar charts mentioned above—had to have a street of sufficiently large dimensions to support it. According to this logic, the "undersizing" of a street, making it too narrow for example, is equivalent to engineering the "collapse" of the city, just as a structure would collapse if its component parts were not large enough to bear the weight of the building. Included in this idea of collapse was also a vision of "economic collapse" of the locality in question, and this added to the compulsion to plan and act in a certain manner.

In the meantime, it is well known that an approach of this sort based on "closed models" makes sense within itself but has the effect of preventing reflection and sealing itself off from criticism.[84] The involved persons set to work, confirmed in their approach by other ideological and social circumstances as well. It was a prevailing conviction of the time that technical organisation represented the way of the future, that it constituted a value-free and apolitical manner of proceeding that produced benefits for all, and that the identified measures in the transport field were mathematically necessary, thus no real choice existed as to whether they should be realised.[85] The undisturbed optimism of the planning engineers of this period can be seen also in the time frames in which they made their prognoses. The year 2000 was the point in time typically found in their projections, a time horizon reaching some 40 years into the future. This was then reduced step by step over the years as the year 2000 remained the typical endpoint of such prognoses for a longer period.

The "traffic loads" shown in the "bar chart plans" seemed to indicate that a street network of greater size was necessary, and this was unquestionably so given the technical assumptions in place. These expansions in the street network had to be made to "handle", "manage", and "master" the coming load.

Against this background in Germany, a large number of so-called "general transport plans" were developed that resulted in extensive modifications and rebuilding in the concerned cities. These activities were necessary to accommodate the planned transport infrastructure also in inner-city locations. These plans were typically accepted as technical specifications in the municipalities without an effective process of public debate. In contrast to new planning for buildings and building areas handled in a public process subject to legal control in zoning and construction plans in Germany, the general transport plans are subject to virtually no public review even today. Often they are simply presented to the elected municipal councils and not formally put to a vote. Nonetheless, they serve as a guideline for administrative actions. They are viewed as the plans and targets of the specialists, and generally there is little doubt as to their validity. In some cases, however, there was opposition to the rebuilding of cities which in the extent of its effect was comparable to a second wave of bombardment. This was particularly so in the more conservative parts of Germany, and in these areas, at least in the inner cities, plans were followed that at any rate preserved the old urban layouts and building lot configurations.

In this situation, a sort of "compromise" was sought that on the one hand preserved something of the old cities and on the other allowed the demolition of many structures and a fundamentally new organisation of the street network. This solution (which hardly deserves to be called such) was articulated in an exemplary form in the expert assessment rendered in Great Britain by the royally commissioned blue ribbon panel in its document "Traffic in Towns". This group was led by Sir Colin Buchanan, active in the Second World War as a combat engineer in the British Army.

Buchanan perfected the principles of shifting traffic from one part of the city to another and separating forms of transport in the traffic flow. The hope to have peace and quiet at one's own domicile and the simultaneous wish to be able to drive without restriction or impediment through a concentrated network of streets and on newly created thoroughfares were combined in the British assessment. Buchanan thus invented the contemporary idea of targeted traffic reduction in certain areas in the form of so-called "environmental areas", as well as the vision of urban expressways that have become a defining element of the urban landscape around the world.

An article in the *Neue Zürcher* newspaper of 29 April 1964 describes the fundamentals of the conception: A system of expressways, constructed as much as possible without intersections, will be established around the inner-city areas. Intersections will be avoided through the construction of traffic cells at the borders of which the streets will end as cul-de-sacs. Within the "cells" it should be quiet as this construction makes it difficult for non-residents to find their way in (or out). The largest "quiet zone" is the pedestrian area, a central shopping district that is surrounded by large parking garages. These in turn can be reached by urban expressways (see Figure 3.11).

As remarked in the *Neue Zürcher*, a striking feature of the concept is an entirely new breakdown of the streets in contrast to the historically developed street network.[86] This new configuration of the network with expressways ("main arteries"), collecting streets and access streets within specific neighbourhoods, was deemed to be more functional. The picture that appears before our eyes here is that of a "machine" called the city and its circulation, which is controlled by technical

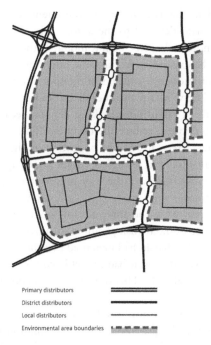

Primary distributors

District distributors

Local distributors

Environmental area boundaries

FIGURE 3.11 Hierarchical plan of distribution streets based on the proposal of transport planner Sir Colin Buchanan, shown here without the outside access routes (drawing: Swen Schneider based on Buchanan's original)

measures that have been designed by specialists. It is therefore no accident that a figure like Buchanan, the combat engineer with experience of war, would be brought in to "solve" the so-called "transport problem".

The logic of this solution works as follows: Bridges or tunnels are built. As with a river crossing in wartime, the most important thing is to ensure that everything has a consistent form and that there is no interruption in forward movement. That means that one system must not disturb another. Thus pedestrians and bicyclists must be moved through the city separately from automobiles.[87] Nearly everything, in fact, is controlled from without and above. Even the inhabitants of the city are no longer deemed to be entitled or competent to decide how their streets will be used. In the interests of ensuring a well-functioning city, the experts are said to know much better what role a street should play than the persons who reside there. Each person is assigned his special position—like audience members in a theatre. The pedestrians have their own protected reserve—the pedestrian zone. Of course, it is surrounded by parking garages as the pedestrians can only reach their zone by automobile. The idea that diverse, multi-faceted exchange between people in their own localities is an integral part of urban transport is assigned to the dustbin of history. Being on foot and in conversation with a companion is now conceived merely as a quaintly appealing aspect of the "shopping experience" in a downtown pedestrian area.

The logic pursued in the British expert assessment leads to an ever steeper growth curve for the areas devoted to the automobile. To keep certain areas of the city "quiet" (i.e. more or less free of automobiles), the street network in other parts of the city has to be expanded. At the same time, through such expansion the attractiveness of the automobile as a means of transportation is reinforced. To gain access to this improved network for automobile transport, more and more vehicles drive on secondary streets, often indeed taking detours because the direct routes have been cut off in an effort to reduce the number of intersections. As a result of these developments, new streets need to be built to make the secondary streets that have now become congested and disturbed "quiet" once again. One expressway after another is built; cities that have three or more such expressway systems are not in the least uncommon.

"I was wrong." These were the three words spoken by the aged Sir Colin Buchanan at a conference of the British planning organisation PTRC in the 1990s. In his planning activities, Buchanan had imagined that the level of automobile traffic on the main streets would be as it had in fact become on the "reduced-traffic" streets within the residential cells. This retrospective statement unfortunately has had little effect until today.

The shifting of traffic away from "residential areas" through the construction of new streets continues to be preached as the best solution for dealing with the inherent conflict between high-speed automobile traffic and pleasant residential living. The unimpeded flow of automobile traffic is still depicted as the mark of a "well-functioning city" or even of a "well-functioning country".[88] It was a false basic logic in which the planners of the 1950s and 60s were ensnared, and it has led to an entirely undesirable form of urban development. Traffic was formerly an integral element of an urban unity consisting of house and street together; it accompanied everyday life. Now it has been declared the enemy, becoming "through traffic", and to master this ever-increasing flow, new streets must be built (although of course not in our own neighbourhoods). The grid of ways through the city—a key quality for those who are attempting to move through the city on foot—has become a system of dead ends (see Figure 3.12).

Was there really—to use a phrase that has become increasingly common as time has gone on—"no alternative" to this development? If one looks today for cities that have remained more or less liveable, one finds some examples of cities in Europe in which a traditional urban grid has been retained at least partially – for whatever reason. For example, the very large city centre of the Italian metropolis Bologna,[89] albeit surrounded by a ring road and various urban expressways, displays the quality and economic attractiveness of a grid-based city. There is Barcelona in Spain. In Germany there are Gründerzeit districts of Bremen, which otherwise is marked by horrendous planning errors, as well as the inner city of Freiburg.[90] However, given the model of city organisation created by Buchanan and copied around the world, it is difficult to find extensive countermodels. Instead what one can observe are faithful examples of the "model" that clearly illustrate its weaknesses. Cities such as Kassel in Germany or Coventry in England are places where

FIGURE 3.12   Orbital motorway (ring road) surrounding the city centre of the
medium-sized English city Coventry. For pedestrians or bicyclists it
is only possible to cross this disproportionately large thoroughfare at a
few selected points—using either bridges or tunnels—to reach the city
centre (photograph: Swen Schneider)

the city centre has become a monofunctional wasteland of consumer shopping.
The residents of the city of Coventry can hardly reach the centre on foot. It is
difficult to cross the expressway streets to gain access to the city centre. At various
points pedestrian tunnels still exist that are highly unpleasant to pass through. The
cities in Europe that have managed to retain the traditional urban grid have not in
the least collapsed, as the planners of the 1950s prophesised. Vitality and diversity
are more what one discovers there; automobile traffic congestion is, in fact, largely
independent of the form and structure of the street network.

The concept formulated by Buchanan in his expert assessment has been very
widely implemented with slight variations. The impact of these changes on the
organisation of the urban street networks in European cities since the 1950s is
typically underestimated in comparison with other factors. This can be seen simply
in the fact that the construction of expressways, bypass roads, and residential areas
separated from the rest of the city continue to be part of the standard repertoire of
urban planning. Together with the separation of functions in the city and an industrially orientated urban model incorporating a vision of the future based on abstract
growth prognoses, the new organisation of the transport network represents a fundamentally important change in the urban environment for its occupants and users.

This new organisation has been strategically pushed forward with the promise
of a relief of the congestion and disturbance arising from automobile traffic. The
obvious losses to the cities in existing structures, green areas, and a historical layout

have always been sold to the public by telling the citizens they will not be affected by automobile traffic if they will only agree to allow new street construction in general (and typically not directly where they live themselves). The effects of automobile traffic that have been experienced up to this time on one's own locality and street should be cancelled out by yet another round of street construction. The individual citizen needn't worry about the growth in the number of automobiles; everyone can drive as much as he or she wishes. In one's own neighbourhood, the prospect of a "quiet and undisturbed" area will be preserved, or so the story goes.

The further significant effect of this planning approach, which creates an urban organisation orientated to large-scale factors, is to deprive residents of access to and control over the streets of their city. Many houses no longer stand directly at a street either because this was not part of the plan when they were constructed or because a new street (or even better a motorway) goes through the city without consideration for existing structures. The basic principle has become the following: Now an engineer, who keeps the urban "machine" running properly, decides what the appropriate function of a street should be. The street before one's front door may be made into a cul-de-sac or into a central axis, all depending on what the engineers decide is best.

By breaking the city into cells and creating traffic reduction zones, fully new forms of city neighbourhoods are created. These are surrounded by central "arteries" like islands in a fragmented urban sea. It is clear that the residents' direct contact and involvement with one another, which in the past came about through movements on foot, will be severely disturbed.

Social Aspects of the Organisation of the City and Transport

A basic prerequisite for a socially effective communal life is the self-determination of the people over their immediate surroundings. It must therefore be considered whether a settlement and its development can be managed by the residents themselves—or not. This relates to a basic question concerning the connection between the city and democracy.[91] This subject is seldom dealt with in urban planning for two reasons:

1. The consideration seems pointless in a way because with a large modern settlement, often referred to as a "metropolis", the factors that can be managed decentrally through direct democratic structures are very limited. Systems for energy, waste management, and transport simply as a result of their great size require a centrally managed, large-scale technical administration.
2. A locality through its style of construction cannot serve up democracy to the people (as in the "doctrine of salvation by bricks", to use Reinhold Niebuhr's distinctive formulation[92]); they must secure it for themselves.

Both of these arguments are at best only partially correct and have had the unfortunate effect that the connections between forms of settlement, democracy, and hegemony in current urban and transport planning are often neglected.

As is so often the case in reality, there are no absolute truths, but the critical issue is what degree of self-determination is possible. If in modern metropolitan settlements and the large-scale facilities that serve them (as with transport for example), the control by specialists seems unavoidable, then the key question becomes: who controls these specialists? There is a further question of whether certain organisational forms of localities impede or facilitate this control. A very important aspect of controllability is the simple size of the bureaucracy and the administrative apparatus. The more extensive, powerful, and complex an administration is (regardless of whether it is private or public), the more difficult it is for the locally concerned people to recognise who is "responsible for them" and, by the same token, to exert influence on the decisions being made or merely to lodge a protest or make a comment at the proper point in the bureaucracy.

The larger and more extensive infrastructure entities become, the fewer are the opportunities for people to have a say. This continues to be the case, although in the meantime countervailing forces to the specialists in the administrative apparatus have succeeded in gaining some rights through the activities of environmental organisations and citizen groups. Motorways, airports, arterial roads, and even high-speed train lines put a burden on people in their immediate vicinity for the benefit of making distant locations more accessible. Decisions regarding such infrastructure tend to be highly abstract and difficult to fully understand, and such decisions are typically made far away from where they are actually carried out.

Just as important as the question of democratic control is the question of who benefits from the decisions to increase the scope of the infrastructure and increasingly orient it to distant locations. The everyday lives of most people—including those living in highly developed industrial countries—are shaped most significantly by the local and regional forms of our settlements and infrastructures. Their daily errands and activities from grocery shopping to work to education take place in the immediate vicinity of where they reside. This also holds true for a large portion of leisure activities as well.

To be sure, the average radius of action for persons has increased enormously in the past century. In Germany, men travel on average 46 km per day, 30 km of this total in the automobile; women travel an average of 29 km per day with 12 km in the automobile.[93] These figures alone show the socially selective effects coming from the promotion and realisation of more and more infrastructure orientated to distant destinations and high-speed travel, which has been depicted in previous chapters here.[94]

First, one is struck by the difference between the figures for men and women. Women's stronger orientation to affairs in the house or flat (as they are for the most part responsible for childcare in the family) and their lower access to an automobile (if "only" one car belongs to a household, it is typically used by the man) produce an action radius for women that is much smaller than that for men. Women's lower income levels also have the effect that women are significantly less mobile than men. The distance travelled per day—and thus the use of distance-orientated transport infrastructure—increases markedly in accordance with the level of income.

A woman from a household with a monthly income of less than €900 travels an average of 19 km per day. This is just slightly over a third of the distance (50 km per day) travelled by a man from a household with an income of €3,600 per month.

These facts stand in stark contrast to the supposed social benefits of new streets or motorways that are typically argued for on the basis of blatantly exceptional "examples". It is the "poor" rural resident who can only find a job in the distant city if a new motorway is built; or in response to extreme congestion the automobile lobby happens to discover its sympathy for a handicapped person who must travel by car and is forced to come too late. Apart from such exceptions, the general reality is of a different order. The transport infrastructure that is orientated to distant locations does not benefit everyone equally; rather it is used principally by male persons from the upper income levels.[95] Because the organisational forms for short-distance connections are at the same time continually neglected, restricted, and devalued through the development of large, long-distance streets, this discrimination against local, small-scale arrangements and connections occurs on a double basis.

And what about the money? Who has paid for these developments? The roadways within town and city limits were taken over by car drivers with virtually no charges made to the new beneficiaries. Even if in Germany the first clause of the Highway Code still contains provisions entitling all persons to equal use of the streets, the roadways in fact serve the occupants of motorised vehicles almost exclusively. The first German motorways were not paid for by car drivers but rather by state resources (which at first often came from profits produced by state-owned rail transport). The initially relatively small number of automobile users in the population (in Germany, only every seventh household owned a car as late as 1960) provided only a minimal portion of the costs necessary to finance the construction of the huge capital investment for motorised transport, whether in the form of motorways or urban expressways. It was an investment of the state and the general public in an imagined future. This start-up support had an enormously strong promotional effect for automobile transport, which without an attractive and suitable network of streets would have been severely limited. This funding was never paid back to the state, and if it were done properly then interest and compound interest would have to be paid. The general public, who predominantly make use of local arrangements and public transport, would have had to receive this money.

The contemporary discussion surrounding whether the automobile should continue to be subsidised from the state budget will only be considered in passing here.[96] Years of political debate in Germany have finally made it generally clear that not even the wear and tear caused by truck traffic on Germany's motorways and streets is paid for by the truck operators themselves. A truck toll on the autobahn has been instituted, but this is in effect paid back to truck operators in other areas through various allowances and abatements. As far as cars for personal use are concerned, it is entirely clear that they do not cover the expenses associated with the enormous ecological damage they are causing (through air pollutants, health injuries caused by noise pollution, and damage to the climate), not to mention the enormous suffering caused by automobiles in the form of deaths and injuries from accidents. These unpaid costs are also subsidies with which the state supports the journey to distant realms.

The people, who primarily make use of and spend time in the immediate area surrounding their place of residence, are subject to three forms of expropriation:

1. They have less and less control over the area immediately surrounding where they live.
2. They pay for and subsidise long-distance transport.
3. They make no substantial use of these long-distance facilities and arrangements.

The various public administration authorities devote their main energies to the development of connections to distant points. By contrast, it has been careful, small-scale planning of houses and their immediate surroundings that has provided the greatest benefits for successful everyday living throughout history. In this process, one thing in particular has become clear: The good organisation of structural and infrastructural features in a local area makes beneficial social processes **possible**. It does not, however, **create** such processes or even influence them as such. On the other hand, bad planning can impede social exchange or in certain cases make it altogether impossible. In the following chapter, an effort will be made to show this concretely and to demonstrate in what manner this has to do with the debate surrounding the issue of "social space", which until now has only been tangentially connected with the issue of transport.

Notes

1 See Kruse, L. 1974.
2 See Proshansky, H. M., Ittelson, W. H., Rifkin, L. (eds.) 1970.
3 An early attempt to integrate spatial considerations can be found in Lewin, K. in: *Psych. Forschung* 19, 1934, pp. 249–299.
4 Worthy of note here is the concept of "Lebenswelt" (world of everyday life) developed by Husserl, which refers to the world in which we naturally and in a sense automatically live. He deals with the life that is led in a "given" space and the effects of this space. Working with these ideas, Heidegger develops important notions regarding the significance of space for life. Later Bollnow, making reference to Minowski, is to be noted. A good summary with references to the persons mentioned here and the corresponding sources is provided by L. Kruse 1970, pp. 27 ff.
5 In this context, see the classic of Simmel, G. 1957, pp. 1–7.
6 See Simmel, G. 1957.
7 See Gesenius, W. 2007, p. 1060 f.
8 See Habermas, J. 1962.
9 See here Veyne, P. 1989.
10 See here and in the following: Vitruv; Baukunst 2. *Band* (in German); translation A. Rode; Zurich and Munich 1987.
11 Reference is hereby made to the (not always identical) use and significance (in comparison to current use) of the corresponding Latin terms in Vitruv's work.
12 Vitruv; Baukunst 2. *Band*, p. 28.
13 See Veyne, P. 1989, p. 335.

14 See Hülbusch, K. H. 1996, pp. 246–251, as well as Hülbusch, I. M. 1978.
15 That is the background of the definition of the street as a row of plazas (see Bäuerle, H.; Theiling, C. 1996) as buildings typically orientated to plazas with their front side. However, even this is sometimes disregarded in planning today as it is often no longer understood that the periphery of a plaza is of great importance for its success. Public discussion of a plaza very often is focused on the centre of the space with competitions for the design of fountains and the like.
16 See Jacobs, J. 1963, p. 27 ff.
17 See Appleyard, D. 1981, p. 21.
18 See Kuhle, D.; Protze, K.; Theiling, C.; Witzel, N. 2004.
19 See Hegemann, W. 1992, p. 218 f.
20 See Bodenschatz, H. 2001.
21 See also Protze K., Theiling, C., in cooperation with Holzapfel, H. 2000.
22 Hippodamus lived in the fifth century before Christ; his participation in the building of Piraeus has been documented. Although his theoretical works are no longer extant, he is cited by Aristotle (see Aristotle, *Politik*, Buch I und II with remarks about social equality). Additional antique cities also point to Hippodamus in their design. However, it is also clear that even older cities had grid street networks or the rudiments of such, for example in the Indus civilisation; see for example Stuart Piggott, 1950.
23 See Jacobs, J. 1963, p. 111 f.
24 In the case of Bremen, an interesting and beneficial "game" is to be found involving the length and breadth of city blocks. The organisation of Bremen residential districts displays oblong city blocks with the shorter side facing the central street and thus a multitude of possible locations for retail establishments.
25 See Protze, K. 2009, p. 33 ff.
26 In some cities of northern Italy, for example in Liguria, this image is to be found in mural form on house walls.
27 See Kuhle, D.; Protze, K.; Theiling, C.; Witzel, N. 2004.
28 See Sieverts, T. 1997.
29 See EVALO 2004, particularly pp. 101–102.
30 See Sitte, C. 2002 (initially 1889); Stübben, J. 1890.
31 See Schivelbusch, W. 1977, p. 158 ff.
32 The novels of Jules Verne (1828–1905) provide just one of many examples reflecting this way of thinking among the educated populace of Europe.
33 In a television programme a critic was heard commenting on the rapid development in Chinese cities: Yes, it is regrettable that the old, small-scale neighbourhood-based forms of urban life are being destroyed by large construction projects, but that could then be repaired in a single step. The expectations during the period of industrialisation in Europe must have been very similar.
34 I.e. determined by (divine) providence.
35 See the discussions regarding the liability laws for the automobile in the German Reichstag, 1909.
36 In Germany there is a museum of the insurance industry in the city of Gotha. According to information to be found there, the first railway accident insurance for passengers was offered in 1853; in 1859 a machine insurance was first offered; in 1898 the first collision insurance for automobiles (but only for collisions between automobiles); from 1902 onwards the first developments towards some form of liability insurance, which was formally implemented in 1909 in the Liability Act for Automobiles.
37 In Germany a detour of 100 metres must be necessary before a violation of the ordinance § 25 section 3 of the Highway Code comes into question. On streets with heavy traffic, pedestrians can only cross over at substantial personal risk should they choose to do so without the benefit of a formal pedestrian crossing. Secured crossings are frequently placed at even greater intervals; in many cases detours of 400 metres or more are necessary.

38 This is also the case in current planning models according to the so-called Shared-Space concept.
39 See Le Corbusier 1962.
40 See Tucholsky, K. 1960 (based on the original from 1929), p. 305 ff.
41 See Hoffmann-Axthelm, D. 1993.
42 With the demand for improved hygiene, which acquired a new topicality following the last major cholera epidemic in Hamburg in 1892, the first strong rationale for welfare-minded city planning came into being. Since this time, public hygiene crops up as the justification for numerous measures, for example the functional subdivision of the city, which have at most only a very indirect connection to health issues.
43 See Strohkark, I. 2001, p. 52.
44 On this point, see Gutberlet, B. 2007, p. 83. This author emphasises the aim of an "effective disciplining" that could be pursued in connection with this instruction for children as well as the opportunity the authorities had to influence the behaviour of other pedestrians.
45 The first traffic sign installed in Germany was a "stop sign" for pedestrians—showing as it were what was to come. With the text "Stop for automobiles", it instructed pedestrians to halt at the edge of the street and allow motorised vehicles to pass. See Fraunholz, U. 2002, p. 62.
46 See Gutberlet, B. 2007, p. 67.
47 Incidentally, this limitation of strict liability was also a model for how nuclear power plants were handled when they were introduced after the Second World War; they also could never have been brought into operation without limitations in strict liability.
48 Association Internationale Permanente des Congrès de la Route. Also see Strohkark, I. 2001, p. 106 on this subject.
49 After the suspension of construction work because of the commencement of the First World War in 1914, the motorway was finally completed in 1921.
50 See Fraunholz, U. 2002, p. 62.
51 On 21 September 1924, the Milan-Laghi roadway was opened for use and is now judged to be the first official highway in Europe. See Strohkark, I. 2001, p. 82.
52 See, for example, Fraunholz, U. 2002, p. 42. Thus the interests of the 2 percent motorised portion of the population stand in opposition to the 98 percent who do not make use of a car.
53 See, for example, Gutberlet, B. 2007, p. 123.
54 See. Gruen, A. 1986, p. 49 f.
55 See Fraunholz, U. 2002, who describes this opposition but cannot fully understand it because he does not address the issue of control of urban space. To the contrary, he emphasises the positive effects of providing new access (through the automobile) without considering the destruction that also occurred in this process.
56 See Fraunholz, U. 2000, p. 232 ff.
57 On this point and in the following, see the descriptions of Steierwald, G. et al. 2005, p. 422 f, in which he nonetheless provides hardly any negative commentary regarding this development.
58 Originally this was viewed quite differently; see Strohkark; I. 2001, p. 183. In the late 1920s a state planning official by the name of Becker from Kassel developed plans for the planting along state roads that were later transferred to the autobahn and expressly identified the purpose of such planting activities as the "protection of vehicles" against the actions of people and animals.
59 See also Steierwald, G. et al. 2005, p. 422.
60 See Feldtkeller, A.; Holzapfel, H. 1999 (or the results of the research project EVALO; on this subject, Holzapfel et al. 2004).
61 See Kutter, E. 1975. Once again confirmed in the final report of EVALO.
62 See Flusser, V. 1998, p. 32 f.
63 See Gröning, G.; Wolschke-Bulmahn, J. 1987.
64 See Bongards 2004, who shows the close connections of Walter Christaller and Konrad Meier to the NSDAP. Meier (NSDAP and SS member from 1931) was named a regular

professor in Hannover after having been sentenced to three years' imprisonment at the Nuremberg trials. Christaller, his subordinate, established important fundamentals for zoning in the Federal Republic of Germany and in Poland (Christaller was a NSDAP member from 1940).

65 See Bernhardt, K. 2003, p. 74.

66 See Bernhardt, K. 2003, p. 22. Reichow was thus active in the SA in addition to being an NSDAP member.

67 See Reichow, H. B. 1948.

68 See Reichow, H. B. 1959.

69 See Reichow, H. B. 1948, p. 71.

70 A communication structure similar to the organisation of transport in Reichow's work is discussed in Flusser, W. 1998, p. 22 as a so-called "pyramid discourse". From a central source (with Reichow the main transport street) there are no intersections on the way to the goal or destination, only branches. This has the effect that only one possible way exists between the starting point and destination (Reichow: no choice of ways). "Examples of this type of structure are to be found in armies, churches and political parties of the fascistic or communist type . . . " (Flusser, V. 1998, p. 22).

71 See here and in the following Lüken-Isberner, F. 1992.

72 The "Gau" was a National Socialist term referring to a regional district in a new administrative structure designed by the Nazis for Germany. It was planned that Kassel would become the capital of one such "Gau".

73 See Durth, W.; Gutschow, N. 1992, in particular p. 212 ff., on the influence of Reichow (the later transport planner) on fascist reconstruction plans during the war.

74 Erich Heinicke, head of municipal planning in Kassel, came into this position in 1941 and remained there until 1949. On taking office, he began with plans for the development of Kassel as "Gauhauptstadt". After extensive destruction of the city in the October 1943 bombing raids, Albert Speer ordered comprehensive plans for the reconstruction of the city in which Erich Heinicke was also involved. The basic assumptions of the National Socialist redesign were transposed by Heinicke and Emile Pohle as a "new reorganisation plan" in the post-war years, but provoked scathing criticism. After a competition was conducted, the reconstruction planning occurred on the basis of an "organic urban recovery". See Durth, W.; Gutschow, N. 1993, p. 286.

75 See "50 Jahre Tempo 50" in the Frankfurter Allgemeine Zeitung, F.A.Z., 3 July 2007, no. 151, p. T6.

76 See Reichow, H. B. 1959. In this role, Reichow is just one of a whole group of actors who wanted to radically change the concept of the Gründerzeit city and replace it with a fully new form of urban layout and infrastructure. See Protze, K. and Theiling, C. 2000.

77 See Alexander, C. 1965, pp. 58–61 (Part 1), pp. 58–62 (Part 2).

78 See Bourdieu, P. et al. 2002.

79 See Leinberger, C. 2007, p. 25.

80 See Leinberger, C. 2007, p. 25.

81 Such models still exist today, often in a more standardised and mathematically and logically improved form. See, for example: Lose, D.; Schiller, C.; Teichert, H. 2006, pp. 181–192.

82 Typically a prognosis is only made for automobile transport, and in some instances for public transport as well. Calculations for pedestrian and bicycle traffic are not made at all.

83 Kurt Leibbrand was convicted of manslaughter against twenty-two persons on 10 January 1966. Twenty-two Italian volunteers from a unit commanded by Leibbrand died under machine gun fire that he ordered in August 1944 after some Italian personnel in the unit had fled. The prosecuting attorney had argued for a charge of murder (which under German law assumes intent). The court judged it to be an instance of manslaughter as the execution order was purportedly issued in a moment of irrationality. The charge of manslaughter had expired under the statute of limitations and Leibbrand went free. See *Die Zeit* 9/1966.

84 See Burckhardt, L. 1974, p. 479 ff.

85 The model of the bar chart plan presented here represents reality in a highly abstracted form and thus distorts the picture of transport, which in fact is a human function, though persons do not appear in the bar chart model in a systematic form. The transport planner, who like all of us is a travelling subject, knows that it is not technical factors that determine traffic and transport flow but human ones (with all the attendant errors and accidents that this entails). But under the influence of this abstraction, he separates himself from his own experience. The destructive effects of such a stance are nicely presented in the psychologist Arno Gruen's book, *Der Verrat am Selbst*, (The Betrayal of the Self), Munich 1986, p. 49 f.

86 Citation from the Neue Zürcher Zeitung 29 April 1964: "The next few generations will have the task of overcoming the shortcomings that derive from the fact that the vehicles of tomorrow are being driven on yesterday's transport network."

87 This concept had great similarity to that of Hans Bernhard Reichow.

88 See, for example, in the German state of Hesse the initiative "Staufreies Hessen" (Hesse without Traffic Congestion).

89 Other Italian cities such as Ferrara or Lucca display similar qualities.

90 Here the inner city is also surrounded by an urban expressway that separates the surrounding metropolitan area.

91 See Battis U. 2008, p. 37.

92 See Jacobs, J. 1984, p. 123.

93 This and the following figures for Germany are from Verkehrsclub Österreich (VCÖ) 2009, pp. 38–40.

94 See Holzapfel, H. 1988, pp. 3–13.

95 See Sachs, W.; Holzapfel, H. 1981.

96 Particularly because in the fiscal crisis of 2009 the subsidisation of automobile transport through auto-scrapping premiums and direct support of the industry is obvious.

4

TRANSPORT AND "SOCIAL SPACE"

The Interaction of Transport Networks and Social Relations

The way in which the interaction between the material organisation of space, as in transport networks for example, and social situations and developments should be analysed is a matter of some controversy, particularly in the social sciences.[1] This controversy extends, in fact, to the question of whether the concept of social space (as used by Henri Lefèbvre[2] for example) can be employed productively in any sense in sociology.[3] This discussion shall not be dealt with in any greater detail here. In the following it will be shown how the everyday possibilities of people are limited by the technical artefacts such as buildings and roads that they encounter in their everyday lives. The urban material space that developed in the course of history through buildings and street networks clearly has limiting characteristics for human and social activity. Nobody can walk through walls; a person living in the ninth floor of a high-rise building cannot check on a child who is playing on the street. In this sense, space can first be understood as a limiting factor for social processes. This approach will be pursued below.

Rudolf Stichweh proposes a similar method of analysing such situations when he writes that in connection with social processes space is a "moment of not easily influenceable exteriority".[4] Social and individual life is certainly significantly affected by this "exteriority". Or to put it differently, the building and planning, the creation of "artificial spaces", and the "control of such spaces" are factors that ultimately figure as constraints for social action.

These instances of "not easily influenceable exteriority" have a further characteristic that is often overlooked. Because they are difficult to influence, they are also exceedingly durable. There are city centres today in Europe that still correspond to the layouts established in ancient Roman times. In the course of history, a tremendous potential in "artificial space" has been developed, together with a huge flood of further potential just in the last century through the advances of the modern construction industry. The organisation of transport networks and buildings determines the daily possibilities of life for people in a decisive fashion, as has already been shown and discussed in previous chapters. On a street where cars drive by at 50 km per hour, I cannot chat with my neighbour; taking a walk outside at an airport is virtually impossible. In the following, it shall be shown that spatial conditions (i.e. the surrounding technical artefacts), which people inevitably become accustomed to and for just this reason often fail to fully discern, have a determining effect on how we live.

To begin with, the place in which a person or family lives very obviously influences the available opportunities and possibilities in life. In addition to the social aspects affecting these opportunities and possibilities, the spatial and structural forms of organisation found in a specific place are also important factors. The Swedish geographer Torsten Hägerstrand addressed these matters from a perspective that focused on spatial and temporal forms of organisation. He developed a model that is relevant not just for geography in which space and time are represented as constraints marking out the limits of action.

Hägerstrand[5] begins with the daily routines of people and the conditions attaching to their places of residence. The patterns of daily activity of a woman in a Swedish city, for example, who takes care of a household with children are characterised by a high degree of regularity. The children wake up, the family eats breakfast, the children go to school on workdays, they come home, lunch is eaten, etc. In such a daily routine there are only limited openings where this woman has the chance to leave her house. These "openings" represent free possibilities for action within the daily routine. As elaborated by Hägerstrand, these limited periods of time only allow for limited activities outside of the house. Such limitations are more pronounced when institutions and facilities must be visited that have their own schedules and organisational constraints, as with the opening times of shops or scheduled lectures at universities, thus establishing further limits. Persons must integrate themselves into a larger organisation of space and time. In addition to these factors, which Hägerstrand calls "coupling constraints", there are natural barriers to using the spatial surroundings of the place of residence (e.g. a person's age, state of health, or handicaps), called "capability constraints" in Hägerstrand's parlance. There are also social limits (e.g. gaining access to certain facilities, clubs, or organisations that are too expensive or exclusive).[6]

The result of these various constraints is the creation of a kind of "island"— Hägerstrand uses the English word in his Swedish text—upon which each person has the potential to move about in his or her daily life. However, progress in transport technology has, according to Hägerstrand, increased the size of these "islands" enormously over the centuries. The airplane with its high point-to-point speed creates foreign archipelagos (to retain the island terminology), expanding the possibilities of action around the place of residence. But Hägerstrand shows his critical stance to increasing distances and speeds in the remarks that follow in his text. On the one hand, he emphasises the possibilities offered by an extension of the action radius of individual population groups, but on the other he points out that the differences between groups in the same area as well as the differences between various areas have already become exceedingly large.[7] To put it simply: As spaces of action grow, so do social differences. This is also true even when people around the world (insofar as they can afford a computer and its connection) can communicate with one another in global data networks. Everyday life persists and the growing social differences continue to have relevance; the computer is in no sense a panacea for the social and political challenges we face.

Hägerstrand's approach of combining the analysis of spatial and temporal organisation to reveal the limits of individual behaviour possibilities has proved to be exceedingly productive in the further development of geography and other sciences. Even today, he can still be seen as a future-orientated scholar. This is particularly so for his later renewed critique of the idea of mobility. This was the basis of criticism of the automobile that developed in the 1970s and of the distance-orientated lifestyle in general. In Germany the works of Hägerstrand are a central basis of the critical transport analysis developed by the Berlin university professor Eckhard Kutter. In the UK, Don Parks and Nigel Thrift have enlarged upon Hägerstrand's ideas. These further developments of Hägerstrand's work show that the increasing speed at which changes in place may be made, particularly as achieved through the automobile, expand the possible living environment for their users, but at the same time constrict the living environment of non-users. This comes about because these increasing distances of travel have a strong effect on the general organisation of space. This effect not only applies to street networks and the immediate surroundings of places of residence, as has been shown in previous chapters, but also extends to establishments such as shops, schools, or administrative offices. As the distance of travel increases, smaller establishments are closed down; larger establishments gain predominance because of the "economies of scale" they provide. The spatial possibilities that are increasing for some social groups through the growing distances of travel are at the same time decreasing for others.

Arguing from very different premises, the environmental critic Ivan Illich introduces the thesis that above a certain speed, which he pegs as slightly above the velocity of a bicycle, the resultant changes affecting a location subject to such levels of speed are generally counterproductive from a social standpoint.[8] This idea—particularly at the global level—is very worthy of consideration. The European or American mode of moving from place to place can certainly not be transferred to India or China. A tourist destination such as Paris, for example, would be filled with Asians (if they travelled in the same proportions as Europeans) wanting to watch a small minority of French people going about their everyday business. The example shows that the volume of overcoming distance currently in place is only possible on a selective basis. The greater the speed and distance of individual persons' travel, the more other people must remain relatively stationary.[9]

Travelling large distances requires large-scale networks on which goods and people can be moved quickly without having to stop. The higher these speeds become, the less they can be controlled by the persons themselves who are in motion. They must be regulated from some exterior agency. With the automobile, this is a familiar process: signs and traffic lights that direct the process of locomotion. These are rules established by third parties, and their general observance is a prerequisite for what is in the best case a relatively safe, high-speed form of travel with the automobile.[10]

Railways served as a model. From the beginning, trains were regulated from without and all the more so with high-speed trains or, for that matter, with airplanes, where the central control determines the whole course of the journey. In such a system accidents can be caused just as readily by the central control (as with errors of the air-traffic control personnel) as by the person who is driving or flying. In rail traffic the removal of the driver in underground trains has been under discussion for some time and is now being put into effect in some instances. In such cases, the vehicles then are exclusively controlled "from without".

The high-speed systems (see Figure 4.1) require not only technical control to operate safely, but also the control of the passengers as they are vulnerable. The higher the energy content and weight of a vehicle, the more susceptible (and inviting) it is to an outside attack or use in an exercise of force. The car bombs[11] used in the modern wars in Afghanistan and Iraq, for example, are not there by accident. Other infrastructure elements for high-speed transport systems are locally vulnerable; railway stations or airports are examples. That the energy content of a jet passenger plane is exceedingly large was proven unforgettably in the attacks of 11 September 2001. This attack was an invitation not only to further acts of violence but also to more extensive control of the users of high-speed transport systems. In

FIGURE 4.1 The city of speed: From the 1920s onwards, technical utopias had an ever greater impact on planning activities (image: Jan Houdek)

air transport between Europe and the USA since, intensive control activities occur with all passengers.

Such control of people corresponds strikingly with the way in which access rights to various facilities are determined by social barriers as described by Hägerstrand. Certain groups of travellers are treated differently from others. They are subject to less stringent controls, their waiting times are reduced.[12] The "normal" passengers are not only subject to intensive control, they are also directed through airports in a highly calculated manner to ensure that they spend as much money as possible.

Philippe Rekacewicz, the illustrator of the magazine *Le Monde Diplomatique*, spoke at the art exhibition documenta XII about the interpretive maps he produces. To the surprise of the audience, he also showed small-scale representations of airports that he had prepared on his frequent journeys. He showed, for example, how the addition of new walls and passageways at the Norwegian airport Oslo effectively forced passengers to go through the "duty-free" shops in the course of the required controls. This is an extreme instance of heteronomous control of small-scale actions, with more than just safety in mind.

Whether it is for genuine or purported safety concerns,[13] the situation that is produced is paradoxical: Precisely these most advanced high-speed transport systems that seem to suggest the ultimate power of the individual determine the actions of their users to a high degree. That may be one of the reasons that the drivers or travellers in such systems become so enraged when these forces become evident. The rage of car drivers who destroy radar speed control equipment with fire bombs is just one example of such behaviour.

The higher speeds and the global networking of transport do not make for greater independence as one might tend to think. Basically, it would seem that overcoming space decreases dependencies. The child who is able to walk away from his mother, the emigrant who leaves her country in search of better opportunities—these are the examples that support such a view. But our examples cited above show that particularly the speed at which a given distance is overcome creates new "islands and exclusions". In transport planning this can at first only be represented as a type of technical limit for human behaviour, an approach for which the works of Torsten Hägerstrand and Eckhard Kutter provide a fruitful basis. This approach could be valuably supplemented by input from the social sciences, which until now have hardly analysed questions of transport. We are in any case still far removed from a "dialectical" or interactive analysis of the realm of technology (in particular, transport technology) and that of social relations.

Besides Lefèbvre, the works of Michel Foucault in particular offer an interesting approach to such questions from the standpoint of the social sciences. Foucault analyses architecture and general spatial arrangements as a means of controlling people. He makes it clear that the way in which we organise space today increasingly serves to facilitate the management and monitoring of the general public making use of these spaces. Large-scale networks, which often concentrate on a single point (for example street networks), tend to limit the degree of freedom rather than opening up new possibilities. He makes it clear, for example, that the possible selection of alternative routes, particularly in small-scale networks, has been substantially reduced in the dominant forms of spatial organisation in modern times.

This of course has much to do with power relations. When the planner Hans Bernhard Reichow models the basic networks of the modern city on the "party cells of the NSDAP", this shows how general forms of control are being realised on a material level. A correspondence of this sort, as has been shown in the preceding remarks, does not occur by chance. A more thorough analysis of these connections is not possible here; it would require an additional book. Unquestionably, however, it is the managers of global capitalism, constantly travelling as they are, in whose interest this control of global space is exercised.

Bigger and Bigger, Further and Further! The Fascination with and Implementation of the Enormous in the Previous Century

No one seems to want to take responsibility now for what has occurred. Many of those who were responsible as planners and "managers of space" for what we have identified as a general enlargement and amplification of scale in urban and transport planning during the second half of the twentieth century say today that they never wanted to have it this way. The process of enlarging facilities, which will be illustrated in detail in the context of Germany in the following pages and which has also occurred in other countries, is rather attributed to the general will of the people and the decisions they have made.

In fact, in Germany it can be shown that it was the planners in leading positions who consistently demanded and then implemented ever larger facilities (from schools to public registry offices) throughout the public sector. For example, it was the planner Gerhard Isbary,[14] working in an instrumental position in the Interior Ministry, who demanded ever larger administrative units to handle the people in a manner that was "economically justified".

Some details regarding Gerhard Isbary (1909–1968): After the end of the Second World War until his flight from East Germany, Isbary administered a large agricultural operation in the Altmark. In 1952 he became a leading administrator of the Institute for Urban Affairs and Spatial Development in Bad Godesberg, and in 1963 he progressed to General Secretary of the German Association for Housing in Cologne. From 1965 he was a technical consultant of the German Landkreistag and in the commission for regional planning of the Federal Interior Ministry.[15] During the Second World War, Isbary was a member of an SS commission that wanted to resettle large parts of the population of Holland in Poland.[16]

Isbary was not an exception. Many of the post-war planners of regional development had already worked in fascist Germany on "large" and "large-scale" projects. As the war had not been won, they worked in the newly formed Federal Republic on a basically unchanged axis concept,[17] focusing on large-scale connections to distant locations or the promotion of large-scale institutions and facilities.[18]

In colonial history it has been shown that the construction of such axes and the development of technologies to overcome large distances were consistently connected with the domination of persons.[19] To be sure, the main phase of imperialism has ended since the 1950s and 60s. Axes thus have gradually lost the aspect of hegemony and domination. They have become one component of a global organisation of space that requires a differentiated analysis. The aim of domination has come to be associated with completely other ideas and has been repressed more and more in general thinking.[20] The new ideas focus on growth and the enlargement of the markets of global companies as well as the superiority of large-scale industrial technology and products in comparison to small-scale forms of labour organisation and production. The basis upon which axis concepts were developed in the mid-twentieth century as well as their connection to modern notions of growth and progress will be outlined in a review of the historical development of these concepts.

Development of Axis Concepts

Pre-nineteenth-century concepts of using long-distance roadways orientated to central metropolitan locations to enable wide-scale access for the purpose of military and political domination (as with Roman roads or the settlement axes of the Baroque period) will not be dealt with in detail. Our focus will be on the explicitly transport-based concepts arising in the period of industrialisation and the developments that then proceeded from these concepts.

The first "axis concept" is judged to be the city layout plan of the Spanish planner Soria y Mata. It was not by chance that he was the founder of the first tram system in the city of Madrid. His plan[21] was based on the technical characteristics of the transport system with which he was so well acquainted. A vehicle that drives at high speeds cannot at the same time turn around lots of little corners. Curves are in any case a problem for trams. A long straightaway is what provides a quick connection for a settlement to the rest of the world, and when everything is organised on a parallel basis then everyone has good access to the transport system. This in any case was the vision and the illusion of Soria y Mata and many subsequent proponents of this view.

It is characteristic of Soria y Mata's approach that he already had ideas of immense axes between Cadiz and Petersburg and even to Beijing.[22] People should live along the central rail/street/infrastructure line. Further removed from this axis, so to speak on the edge of the residential ribbon, leisure areas and rural life should find a place. This represented an early "Fordist" concept, which made the assembly line (already existing in manufacturing) into the centre of an idealised settlement. The "ribbon city" should provide the advantage of a high degree of accessibility to distant locations and at the same time provide easy access to a rural idyll. Even today there are authors who wonder why this form of urban settlement did not come to predominate. One disadvantage of this form of locality is clearly its dependence on large-scale technical infrastructure. Likewise, the promise of equal accessibility along the length of a single axis is based on a thoroughly mistaken assumption.

At the beginning and in the course of the last century, the axis or ribbon city was the subject of various visions, elaborations, and variations. One impressive example is the 1910 concept of the "Roadtown" of the American urban planner Edgar Chambless. The inhabitants of the city would live above an enclosed infrastructure consisting of a street and a sort of urban subway. In this type of street house they would have direct access to transport, according to the vision of the planner. The structures of the city should extend as a boundlessly long house from the existing end station of the municipal rail lines outward into the countryside.[23] Edgar Chambless even planned to establish a limited stock corporation and announced the imminent construction of his ribbon of settlement with a street and urban rail line at an underground level. His vision was never realised, however. Chambless had clearly made a false calculation. Why, given cheaply available land in the environs of the cities, would it make sense to use a form of construction that saves space but is highly expensive with streets constructed underneath the houses?

Chambless' plan also reveals another problem of the ribbon city theoreticians. It is simply not correct to assume that all persons living on the same axis have the same advantages. The long ribbon-like house of Chambless' vision would have a train station every 1 to 2 kilometres. A person living in the middle between two stations must walk 500 to 1000 metres to get to the next train stop, paying for the rail connection under his domicile but with reduced benefits. With long-distance rail connections with larger intervals between the stations, this problem is still more pronounced.

While Chambless' plan failed due to the costs of his "invention", various radical new means of access to municipal centres were planned and in fact built. Initially there was only occasionally an integrated planning approach including both public transport and urban development, even though the advantages of facilitating the settlement of the environs of cities (with ever-increasing density of population) were recognised early by planners.[24] By the 1920s, concepts for the development of rail lines into the city centres were explicitly combined with concepts of settlement development.[25]

In Germany, the architect and planner Fritz Schumacher presented plans for Hamburg and Cologne featuring axes of settlement orientated to the centres of those cities. The basic structure for these settlement axes was provided by rail lines. The idea of these concepts was to encourage the growth and enlargement of manufacturing and administration in the involved localities. The transport systems allowed the establishment of expanded and more transport-intensive facilities. The masses of the working population could be mobilised in even greater accumulations than before, making it possible to increase the revenues and profits of the capitalist businesses operating on the market. Looking back on these developments, they in no way represented a "voluntary" or "freely taken" decision of the people to engage in a process of suburbanisation; rather, this was a planned process in which the constraining factors of prices and available resources often allowed persons no other choice but to move to the suburbs. Similar processes of suburbanisation also occurred in many other European cities such as Paris and London in the early 1900s. In Germany, following an initial phase during which this process of suburbanisation was determined by the construction of rail lines, this development was interrupted. Then with the advent of fascism, the old imperial idea of demonstrating and exercising direct dominance by the development of axes was taken up again.

In the ideas and images of futurism in Italy, trains and transport infrastructure played a central role. (The Italian fascist Mussolini also adopted ideas from this source.) The long straightaways of a rail line embodied the affinity futurist artists had for high-speed formations.[26] Similar instruments of design were also used by Le Corbusier whose previously mentioned "Plan Voisin" for Paris also included a long straight axis for automobiles as a central element. The straightaway pointing to a distant destination is a characteristic feature of streets, railways, and also the first motorways; for fascism, it also became a symbol of power.

In Germany, Albert Speer planned an enormous straightaway axis for Hitler in Berlin, the so-called North-South Axis, which should culminate in a "Hall of the People" in which 150,000 to 180,000 people could congregate. The authors Hans Joachim Reichardt and Wolfgang Schächse provide a telling description of the construction activities undertaken to this end. Their aim is not only to describe the madly monumental scale of the buildings and the supporting transport axis, but also to reveal the social and political implications of such an undertaking. They make clear that simply for the preparation of the construction of the monumental edifice and the attendant infrastructure and access roads, an almost unbelievable effort was required. It was necessary to demolish a whole district of the city and expel large numbers of residents from their homes, as well as to undertake huge efforts to acquire the necessary building materials (Hitler and Speer insisted on natural stone). With the knowledge and evident approval of Speer, buildings planned for demolition were initially cleared through the forced eviction of Jews and later through their arrest and deportation in concentration camps, where they were subsequently subject to mass murder. The building materials were brought by the SS from quarries at the concentration camps, but Speer regularly complained about the quality of the materials provided.

Large central axes and facilities not only symbolised dominance, they also required it. If the North-South Axis in Berlin had been completed, then the maintenance of the gigantic hall (everything from lighting to waste disposal systems) by itself would have also generated enormous ongoing costs. The plan was to finance such activities through the losers of the war.

Another entirely ludicrous plan for the construction of elaborate new axes was the so-called broad-gauge railway between Berlin and Rostow am Don, with branches to Hamburg, Munich, and Linz as well as other connecting lines. The plan involved constructing a railway with a width of 4 (and later 3) metres. The plan was pursued with very intensive activities starting in 1942 until the end of the war, despite the competing outlays for war planning and investments.[27] By the end of the war, almost everything was ready for the railway from the design of the railway cars and locomotives to the first test line. Hitler continued to brood over problems of station planning for Linz and Munich even as the shots of Russian artillery were to be heard in Berlin.

Extreme examples of this sort show what was intended with transport axes of such enormous dimensions; after Russia was conquered, the riches and raw materials of the annexed lands were to be brought to Germany. This was all pushed forward with great energy and highly detailed planning, but ended of course in ruins. It was, however, an important basis and the historical inheritance of urban and transport planning in Germany in the 1950s, 60s, and 70s.

The continuity of the people active in these areas before and after the Second World War in the western part of Germany was remarkable. Road builders and engineers apparently were seen as being beyond suspicion, although many of them had been Nazi Party members. Nonetheless, they continued to be employed, some of them in high government positions with substantial management responsibilities. Prof. Alfred Böhringer, for example, belonged to the NSDAP from 1933 and worked with Alfred Speer in the Reichsministerium under Hitler. In 1946 he moved directly to a position in road construction in the state of Baden-Württemberg and rose through various positions to be in charge of all transport policy by 1964. Böhringer is just one example of others such as the already-mentioned Hans Bernhard Reichow or Kurt Leibbrand, who had a leading role in shaping the development of the West German system of roads and streets from 1945 to 1970.

It is understandable that specialists were in high demand for the reconstruction of the destroyed transport networks after the war. Nonetheless, it is astonishing how little attention was given to the earlier political role these persons had played. In the course of the fascists' construction activities in the final years of the war, for example in Norway close to the Arctic Circle where roads were built, thousands of persons perished (mainly prisoners of war used for forced labour) without any of the involved engineers ever being called to account. Instead, nearly all of them moved on to have prominent careers. In their work, the propensity to gigantism and projects of enormous scale continued. Frequently, the plans used had been prepared before 1945.

The continuation of large-scale planning and the compulsion to construct huge facilities in industry and in state building were justified in a completely different fashion after the war. In Germany prior to the end of the Second World War, such efforts served as a demonstration of the power of the National Socialist government and supported the mass production of weapons. After the war, this scale of development was justified as a means of promoting economic development and the growth of modern industry.[28] In many cases (the transport sector again is a clear example), large-scale facilities built according to Hitler's plans directly became the site of capitalist mass production, as with the Volkswagen factory in Wolfsburg, for example.[29] The VW factory was intended to export cars to the countries of the victors of the Second World War. To be sure, functionally and technically modern elements were part of the fascist way of thinking. Nonetheless, it is surprising how seamlessly the successful operation of large-scale structures and facilities established in Germany under fascism could be continued after the war.[30]

With the new argumentation, the enlargement of industrial facilities and institutions as well as the erection of large-scale transport systems ("axes") became an important goal in Germany. The fitting and expansion of factories for large-scale production was a determining factor for the economic re-emergence of West Germany in the 1950s and 60s. The developers and planners who supported and implemented these facilities and the corresponding large-scale infrastructure (as with large-scale transport axes) were often the same persons as before 1945, now with a new rationale behind their endeavours. In West Germany the autobahn network destroyed during the war was reconstructed first, concentrating on the north-south connections. Soon afterwards, central motorway connections in the area of the Rhein-Ruhr industrial zone and in other economic centres were expanded. All of this occurred once again without financing from car drivers—at least initially.

Even in 1960, only one in seven households in West Germany owned an automobile, with a correspondingly low level of tax revenue from automobile owners. Rather it was general tax revenues (including at that time the profits of the German Railway) that were invested in the development of the motorway network. This financing was available because, in contrast to the period following the First World War, West Germany did not have to pay reparations for the damages caused by Germany during the war. Rather, some time after the end of the war, it began to receive considerable aid from the USA which needed West Germany to serve at the front line in the "Cold War" against East Germany as part of the Soviet bloc.

In the cities of the new German Federal Republic, the reconstruction was conducted in more and more locations in accordance with the plans of Hans Bernhardt Reichow and later those of Sir Colin Buchanan. At the same time, distant locations outside of the cities could be reached increasingly quickly principally with the automobile or by lorry. This in turn allowed existing large-scale industrial facilities to expand even more, as the catchment areas for the distribution of goods and for commuting employees also grew. When more people can reach a new supermarket at the edge of the city in the same amount of time as before, the supermarket has a basis for expansion. A factory that supplies goods to an area initially with ten distribution centres is able to supply the same area with just seven and later with five consolidated centres with shorter travel times and substantial savings.

The fact that the increase in revenues for such large facilities was accompanied by the disappearance of smaller businesses and manufacturing sites, and that the larger distances travelled create "external costs" such as noise or exhaust emissions, was initially hardly addressed. A development into a "country of great distances" was subsidised indirectly on an economic basis and this subsidisation achieved its goal: everything became larger! Large facilities of this sort have their own fascination. A gigantic shopping centre inevitably makes an impression on customers who until then were only acquainted with smaller establishments, simply on the basis of its enormous dimensions.

The developers and planners in Germany—despite their later protestations that all their countermeasures simply hadn't availed of anything[31]—promoted the new developments in any way they could. A larger facility was said to be better for the customers as well as for the economy as a whole. The benefits of such economies of scale, i.e. the fact that a larger factory has lower per piece costs, were seen as a rule that could be just as well applied to services or government administration. In Germany it was particularly the planner Gerhard Isbary, who had already made a name for himself with large-scale planning under fascism, and the planner Erika Spiegel, influential into the 1990s, who praised large-scale facilities.

Spiegel characterised the development in this manner:

> For some years now it can be seen that for each distinct functional area so-called centres are coming into existence. This started with shopping centres, and then was followed with culture centres, sports centres, educational centres, church centres, healthcare centres, leisure centres, wholesale centres and much more. Rationalisation through improvement of internal processes and better utilisation of technical and organisational infrastructure are central aspects of this development. In addition there are advantages for the users of such facilities who are presented with a diverse set of offerings and the resulting possibilities for comparison 'under one roof'.[32]

Another justification for this tendency to enlarge facilities, particularly in the public sphere, purports that the "functions" in question demand operations on a larger scale.

> It stands to reason that the businesses serving private economic needs depend on the purchasing power of a certain number of inhabitants to ensure a secure basis for their business. With public facilities, the economic aspects are less predominant and normative claims come to the fore. In this situation the 'functional size' is the critical factor, i.e. the most advantageous size which is determined after assessing all relevant aspects and critically evaluating all requirements of a particular facility.[33]

What is meant by "functional size" becomes clear very quickly when one looks at the tables in which they are specified. For a cemetery, for example, in a particularly noteworthy instance, Edmund Gassner judges the necessary population base to be between 80,000 and 100,000 for "full utilisation and optimal operating efficiency", conceding nonetheless that in the event of a "more scattered structure of settlement" one could go below this value.[34]

Cemeteries, schools, kindergartens—everything became larger. This "basic structural transformation" was strongly supported by the initial proponents of axis concepts. Larger facilities, particularly when they are also more specialised in the services they provide, require larger catchment areas. The customers come from greater distances as well as the suppliers for more diverse offerings in a specialised segment. Isbary remarked on an "era of increasing integration" at an early date;[35] this should likewise be accompanied by a "total restructuring of the realm of being".[36]

This restructuring can best be described by the term "enlargement of scale", which was also used by the protagonists of this development. A comprehensive concept emerges from this approach. A demand is made to increase the size of administrative units in the state and society to meet the larger scale found in other facilities. Who should plan and administer these larger schools, swimming centres, shopping centres, etc.? Gerhard Isbary[37] detected an "inability of many localities to fulfil their basic (administrative) duties" and he proposed to consolidate the localities into larger regions. This initiative was taken up in many cases in Germany in regional and administrative reforms in which such larger administrative units were in fact created.

The idea of "increasing integration", also shaped by Isbary, of course entails a need for larger infrastructure elements in the whole transport and supply area. A few large facilities in contrast to many smaller facilities require concentrated energy and water supplies and similar changes in the provision of transport. All of these facilities must be planned on a larger scale.

To summarise: Larger facilities and larger administrative units are—purportedly—necessary due to "functional requirements". The separation of the functions of labour, recreation, and leisure, originally developed as a concept for the city, is now subjected to a "scale increase". Entire regions are now devoted to the function of recreation (in addition to agriculture) when they cannot afford other functions.[38]

Such large facilities in the "land of enlarged scale" did encounter criticism. The arguments of the German-born British author Ernst Friedrich Schumacher presented in his 1973 work *Small is Beautiful* received considerable attention. On the basis of a comparison of Buddhist principles and the "giganticism" of the institutions and facilities in the capitalist systems, Schumacher commends small-scale arrangements. His various works provide ideas that even today serve as a basis for the economics of sustainability. Together with such later writers as Klaus Traube and Otto Ullrich in Germany, he sees large-scale technology as an instrument of domination over nature and mankind.[39] Central points of this critique include the following:

- Large facilities, factories, and energy supply units create societal power centres that are difficult to control and that promote dependence.
- Large facilities create a drive to establish other large facilities and are thus part of growth economies. How would it be if economies were to shrink?
- Large facilities tie up societal capital in huge volumes for long periods of time. They cannot react flexibly to changing developments and changing wishes of the people. In effect, they "cement" the future.
- Large facilities (such as shops and supermarkets) seem to increase the range of choices. In fact, they result in a faux diversity of standardised articles of great similarity with mass production.[40]
- Large facilities (for example schools) often lead to anonymity and bureaucratic forms of organisation.
- Enormous facilities are as a rule the cause of a correspondingly enormous volume of automobile traffic!

The growth in traffic and transport in the 1960s and 70s in the western industrialised states cannot be attributed simply to the development of the transport routes and the rebuilding of the cities. The increasing size of all industrial facilities and public institutions and the increasing division of labour and specialisation created a further cause for this expansion.[41] This development of having more and more streets with ever heavier traffic is reinforced by other influences: Large industries have a strong influence on political decisions. Such industries are dependent on streets and traffic and use their influence to demand increased road construction from the government. This phenomenon can be tracked in many western industrialised states in the political context.

A widespread error whereby cause and effect are confused serves to strengthen this influence. Because the growth of large facilities and the establishment of new facilities results in a growth of transport and particularly of automobile use, it is concluded that building up the transport network automatically results in economic growth.

It has been shown above, however, that an enlargement of scale of this sort and making transport easier and cheaper promotes a continuing enlargement of facilities and centralised industries. The growth that takes place here is generally not in quality, but most certainly in the consumption of raw material, in particular petroleum products. Small and medium-sized establishments tend to be the losers in connection with such developments. The growth of larger establishments on the other hand leads to increased levels of transport, which can only be financed through continued growth. An upward spiral is set in motion in which there is an economic necessity to have more and more growth, leading to a further necessity of having more cars and streets, which makes for a form of development that is not at all sustainable.

The Accelerated and Unrestricted Development of Transport Infrastructure and the Apogee of Fordist Planning

Until approximately 1960, the growth of automobile transport and the establishment of a motorised society seemed still to be visions for the future, but then suddenly things changed very quickly. In a "breathtaking rush",[42] West Germany rose to become the second largest automobile producer of the world. In 1956, 1 million vehicles were produced; in 1962 it was already nearly 2.5 million.[43] The changing spatial conditions, intensive advertising, and the quite real advantages accruing to the first car drivers resulted in an enormous rise in car purchasing among the population. The decisive stimulus for an accelerated development in the transport infrastructure came in 1963 in Germany when for the first time traffic congestion occurred on a German autobahn.

Up to this time, the growth in traffic was well under the existing capacities of the street network. In the expansion of the direct motorway connection to Scandinavia and the motorways leading into this route, an 8-kilometre stretch in the vicinity of Neustadt in Schlewig-Holstein was more or less "forgotten". On top of this, the summer school holidays were scheduled in an unusual manner, sending many drivers on their summer holidays at the same time: this resulted in the first large-scale motorway traffic jam in Germany. The echo of this occurrence was enormous. At the front of the media pack was the then highly influential news magazine *Der Spiegel*, with a cover story titled "Speed Limit 20 km per Hour".[44] The article presented this first traffic jam in 1963 as a genuine affliction and compared it with calamities such as a fire or flood. In painstaking detail the magazine specified all of the aspects of the event including additional small delays and the length of the various instances of backed-up traffic. The article recounted the fates of various drivers such as that of a miner from Witten who was travelling to the funeral of his mother and arrived late due to the congestion, appearing at the cemetery as the grave was being filled – a personal calamity.

The transport authorities and ministers in Germany were very quickly made responsible for the situation; apparently they had not acted in accordance with the people's requirements. The magazine demanded a significant increase in funds for road construction and better management of construction sites. Although Germany at this time had the most motorways of any country in Europe, crude comparisons (at least in the cited *Spiegel* article) were made with the situation in other countries (e.g. regarding the total length of all streets) that indicated that Germany was inadequately equipped with roadways.

From this time on it was no longer the state that built streets to fulfil a vision of the future; rather, the politicians were driven by the demands coming from the general population and from the media as in the *Spiegel* article quoted above. The prerequisites and subsidies implemented by the political system and society in effect forced the people to embrace the car. Even in the official government prognoses of the 1960s and 70s, the actual demand of the population for automobiles tended to be underestimated.

In Germany, Georg Leber, a Social Democrat, took over the office of transport minister after the departure of Hans-Christoph Seebohm, who had had limited success in the position since the first autobahn traffic jam. Leber accelerated the development of the transport infrastructure as much as he could, and it is interesting to see how he used social democratic argumentation to support this new and unprecedented level of road construction. He assumed that broader portions of the population, in particular production workers and office employees, should be able to have their own automobile to achieve social equality with those who already possessed such vehicles. The promotion of the automobile for all socioeconomic classes in the society was supported as a way of creating social equality. This was also reflected in legislation regarding regional planning in Germany which required that access be provided to the autobahn or other fast road connections throughout the entire country, to ensure "equal living conditions" in all localities.

The project undertaken by Transport Minister Leber that is best known today is the so-called "Leber Plan". Leber formulated the vision in a speech in which he stated that every German citizen should have access to the autobahn at no greater distance than 20 kilometres. In fact his plan, which was presented to the Bundestag at the end of the 1960s, was much more complex. In particular, he was concerned with reducing the amount of lorry traffic on the roadways to ensure there was adequate space for the new drivers in other socioeconomic classes to make use of their newly acquired automobiles. This part of his plan, however, was a complete failure because it was in direct opposition to the interests of the growing economy, which was marked by a growing degree of differentiation in the production process.

In addition to the general enlargement of manufacturing facilities, factories were also beginning to concentrate more narrowly on one segment of the production process so that the so-called vertical range of manufacture declined. Reduced vertical range in manufacturing means that more half-finished goods from other factories must be supplied to complete the production process. The trucking lobby in Germany had already become very powerful in the 1960s. When lorry transport was unavailable at that time, many factories very quickly had problems with unavailable components and raw materials, despite extensive warehousing of supplies.

Leber's plan to increase the costs of lorry transport and reduce the amount of lorries on the roads in favour of rail transport met with no success.[45] With his plans, which are remembered not for the initiative against lorry transport but rather for the promise of equal access to the autobahn, began the engaged effort to "master" the growing traffic volume through a corresponding growth in road construction. Although *Der Spiegel* had already remarked in 1963 that autobahn construction had little effect on unemployment (the wage portion of such investments even at that time was only 20 percent), autobahn construction was repeatedly used by various governments as an economic stimulus in times of stagnating growth.[46]

Between 1963 and 1990 the German autobahns tripled in length, not including the significant widening of many sections and the increased number of driving lanes. In addition, there was a significant build-up of existing federal through roads (Bundesstrasse). In total more than 4,000 km of federal through roads with a width of 11 to 20 metres were created, roadways that frequently had four lanes and were similar to an autobahn in their effect. Each new roadway also created more traffic as the attractiveness of the automobile transport system as a whole increased. As a result, even these enormous construction undertakings lagged behind the growth in automobile traffic.

A "Germany without traffic jams", as was regularly promised by transport ministers, was not brought into being as a result of these activities. What did result were significant changes in the structure and distribution of settlement in Germany that went beyond the enlarged size of various facilities, which has already been discussed. Individuals making decisions about where to live and where to build new houses also contributed to the growth of distances in general transport. While the accessibility of suburban locations improved with the road construction measures, problems in the city centres were increasing. The General Transport Plans of the 1960s and 70s were soon no longer able to cope with the volume of traffic generated in urban centres by the new autobahns and expressways.

In addition to the measures coming from the works of Hans Bernhard Reichow and Sir Colin Buchanan, many cities endeavoured to increase the space available for motorised transport. Often bicycle paths and pedestrian walkways were removed or no longer built in new constructions as the automobile became the central focus of urban planning. As a result of these developments, the strain of urban living increased enormously. Noise and air pollution increased significantly. The possibilities of shopping on foot in one's immediate neighbourhood, or of relaxing on a balcony or on the street in front of one's home, decreased markedly. People moved to the quieter and more pleasant suburban areas and ever further from the city centres.

The expansion of automobile transport promoted urban sprawl and the formation of the "Zwischenstadt" or the "city in between". The Berlin planner Eckard Kutter described this very accurately as a "vicious circle of transport planning".[47] The traffic within the cities increases as a result of continually improved connections with the surrounding area. The people move into this surrounding area. As a result of their commuting to jobs in the city centres, traffic increases. This in turn leads to a further exodus of persons from the urban centres and further requirements for road construction. The centres of cities in Germany and elsewhere in Europe are shaped by this vicious circle and its consequences. In the morning and evening rush hours, when people are commuting to work, the roads are very full over a long period.

The relevance and significance of the urban centre are also being transformed through changing forms of accessibility and the creation of numerous expressways in and around the cities. Locations at motorway junctions have become attractive for supermarkets; factories and craft enterprises move to the urban fringe. Such decentralised locations are also more difficult for public transport to serve as it is more suited to the classic concentrated form of the city. This leads to additional reinforcement of car-based transport.

The heavy traffic load in the cities and then on the urban expressways and bypasses prompts people to dream of some sort of relief. This is sought in the peace and quiet of a single-family house based on the model of single-family housing tracts in the USA, a form of settlement that has spread to more and more stratums of the population in Germany. In the 1960s it was initially the more affluent classes that could afford to move away from the city centre. From the end of the 1960s and moving into the 1970s, the construction of single-family houses has been promoted with targeted subsidies. Also in this connection, it was social democratic governments that aimed to provide production workers and office employees with the opportunity to "live in peace and quiet".

The basis of such thinking was, as before, the functionalistic image of the city as formulated in the Charter of Athens. The workers and employees should only perform their work-related tasks at the workplace and then have the chance to "revive" without stress and strain in the residential areas specially designed to allow this. In other urban areas, with the urban centre as designed on the model of Sir Colin Buchanan's plans, shopping should take place in pedestrian areas. That this functionalised image of the city with residential areas, industrial areas, and a shopping zone produces a high degree of monotony in the overall urban setting was not apparent to the involved planners; and this was not the only effect. The traffic grew and grew through the expansion of single-family housing areas which featured a low density of settlement and typically two-car garages.

Collectively, this leads to a growth in the distances travelled and in the volume of traffic. Soon the northern-most expressway of one city is not far removed from the southern-most expressway of the next locality. The urban model of functional separation was soon applied on a regional basis. The residential and shopping areas are quickly surrounded by overcrowded streets when they are not far enough away from a city, and when they are further removed, the expressways and autobahns soon envelop them. This produces "fragmented regions"[48] as described by Andreas Thaler and Matthias Winkler, regions that are orientated to further growth but that have completely lost the urban qualities of proximity described in the first sections of this book.

The fragmented region consists of isolated islands within which the residents can move; however, beyond the confines of such islands the use of a motorised vehicle is necessary. The fragments are dependent on one thing above all: petroleum as the fuel for motorised vehicles. From the 1970s, criticism of these developments from the so-called ecology movement began to be articulated. This is the subject of the following chapter.

Critical or "Alternative" Transport Planning in Germany since 1970

In the so-called student movement of 1968, there was a central contradiction. Many of the principal actors in the movement came from the middle class but were inspired in Germany and elsewhere in Europe by Marxist theory that maintained that the "working class" was oppressed and that its rights must be strengthened. In some countries in Europe, this movement led by middle-class intellectuals also found support in the labour unions and in broader sections of the population (particularly in France and Italy). In general, however, and particularly in West Germany, it was a fact that despite the distribution of literature by students at the factory gates, interest in Marxist ideas remained relatively slight in most large factories and businesses.

It came about quite naturally that a portion of the persons politicised in the student movement (if only because of their social origins) eventually directed their attention away from the production sector of the economy to the "reproduction sector", and looked to see how a similarly inspired critique could be applied to the living conditions found in residential areas and in the cities. A manifesto by A. Mitscherlich, "The Inhospitality of Our Cities—Incitement to Strife", appeared in its first edition in 1965 and was an initial instance of such criticism in Germany. At first it generated only limited interest, but by 1969 the work had appeared in its sixth edition and had been printed more than 50,000 times.[49] For a work situated between psychology and city planning, this was an impressive printing.

In his book, Mitscherlich points to the bad configuration of workplaces at companies and the difficult competitive conditions existing there, placing this situation in juxtaposition to the unvarying monotony of residential conditions in modern blocks of flats. He describes how the inhuman planning of residential areas renders democratic communication and genuine freedom illusory goals in the society.[50] From an urban planning standpoint, Mitscherlich's work was not highly developed and his critique of functionalism was not so clearly articulated, but large parts of the work nonetheless dealt with how ill-advised urban planning forces people into destructive living conditions. Child-rearing was a particular focus for him. He advocated the creation of denser networks of playgrounds that were safe from traffic, better access to green areas, and more employees at kindergartens.[51]

Mitscherlich's essay was an important starting point for "alternative" city and transport planning in Germany. For the middle-class protagonists of the student movement, the automobile actually tended to have a positive role. One typical feature of the hippie movement was the Volkswagen bus painted with flowers. Without the widespread availability of cars among the middle-class adherents of the movement, the outdoor rock festivals on farmland and in rural settings couldn't have been staged as they were. In the critique of the living conditions in residential areas, the negative effects of the automobile such as noise, exhaust, and air pollution soon also became an issue.[52]

In Berlin, where the student movement was particularly strong, a "Citizens' Committee for Transport Policy" was established in 1972, and drew attention with its first actions against increasing automobile traffic (the first two bicycle demonstrations occurred on the Kurfürstendamm in Berlin, but only attracted 150 and 90 persons, respectively). A broad movement of rejection developed, in particular against the "Westtangente" urban expressway in Berlin. This led in 1974 to the founding of the first large citizens' initiative dealing with transport issues, the still extant "Westtangente" group. They turned their energies against the construction of a planned north-south city autobahn that would pass through the districts of Schönenberg and Charlottenburg. The criticism grew increasingly intense from 1975 onwards and gained more and more support so that soon thousands of signatures had been collected and bicycle demonstrations were also attended in similar numbers.

This initiative was a model for more and more opposition that spread across Germany to new motorways and other transport facilities such as airports. In 1976, the first book of the citizens' initiative, "West-Tangente", was published: *City Expressways—A Black Book for Transport Planning*.[53] The criticism of individual city expressways gradually coalesced into a general critique of increasing reliance on the automobile and the consequences of such an approach on the environment.

By the end of the 1970s, proponents of alternative models began to formulate their ideas following the initial protest movement against new roadways. These ideas included visions of cities with lower speed limits and car-free cities, as well as proposals to change automobile technology to produce smaller and slower vehicles.[54] With the founding of the ecological party "Die Grünen" (the Greens) in Germany, these ideas also acquired an essential political expression. In the area of non-governmental organisations, the organisation Greenpeace dedicated itself to promoting alternative ideas in opposition to an ever-increasing number of motorways for the transport future.

A kind of "alternative" discipline of transport planning emerged on this basis. The concerned public action groups organised regular congresses and in transport studies, the first groups of scholars were established that criticised the growth of car use in society. The connection of urban planning with questions of transport and the development of a vision of a "city of short distances" were particularly the focus of the Berlin transport planner Eckhard Kutter and soon also his Viennese colleague Hermann Knoflacher, who each held professorships in transport planning.

In Germany, the so-called "first energy crisis" in 1973 resulted in the imposition of a speed limit of 100 km per hour on motorways and 80 km per hour on ordinary roads for nearly a year, and at the high point of petroleum shortages this also resulted in a policy of car-free Sundays. These developments gave the alternative movement an additional boost. On the other hand, it soon became clear that the automobile industry particularly in Germany was (and is) a strong opponent of such initiatives. After the first oil crisis, the new speed limits were rescinded. Today it still has not been possible for "alternative" transport planning to implement a general speed limit on German autobahns. The demands of action groups and alternative scholars for such a limitation were soon met with opposition by organisations of the automobile industry and the insurance industry, which accepted a portion of the demands but placed them in an entirely different context. It was once again the context provided by the Charter of Athens.

In Germany the insurance industry and its offices of transport research (maintained by the HUK Association) took a leading role in developing this argumentation. These forces accepted a decrease in speed limits in "purely residential areas", but they only wanted to allow this on a selective basis in connection with physical changes in the street design. This debate about so-called "traffic-calming" measures shaped the public discussion in Germany from the mid-1980s onwards.

Alternative transport planning and accident researchers showed that under the speed of 30 km per hour, pedestrian accidents resulted in significantly fewer fatalities. Head injuries were a particularly important criterion.[55] In the ensuing political debate in Germany, however, the representatives of the HUK Association carried the day. Politicians supported the approach that car drivers should be informed of the 30-km speed limit through clear physical indicators in the street design. This also quickly gained the support of the automobile industry so that it was ensured that the 30-km speed limit would not be imposed on a general basis, but rather could only be used in a few very limited urban situations and in exclusively residential areas. The automobile business thus had succeeded in keeping their product in the dominant position on broad sections of the urban landscape.

The new transport planning approach had gained sufficient influence in many municipalities and also at the state level in Germany, so that in the German Association of Cities and Towns it was decided that a general 30-km speed limit should be in force, except when otherwise noted for explicit exceptions on main thoroughfares and rights of way. Without any large construction measures, this proposal would have established a zone covering approximately 80 percent of the roadways within German municipalities where a general speed limit of 30 km would be in force.

The supporters of a case-by-case solution were victorious, however, and they also received support from portions of the new alternative, green-orientated transport planning forces. A significant portion of this alternative movement came from the bourgeois middle and upper class and thus had often grown up in just such "purely residential" areas. Impressed by initial traffic-calming solutions from Holland that featured brightly coloured pavements and speed reduction humps that gave such residential areas a "nice feeling", portions of the new transport planning forces were also favourably disposed towards new examples of street reconstruction that forced cars to slow down through structural measures.

It did not become evident to many persons involved in these discussions that the classic division of the street, whereby a safe front yard is created by means of a pedestrian pavement in front of the houses lining the street, is lost with such an arrangement. The "traffic calmers" postulated a mixed-use street area in which pedestrians, bicyclists, and playing children could make use of the street with equal rights. In Germany a sign was adopted in the traffic regulations that showed playing children in front of a house and indicated equal status for pedestrians and car drivers as well as a lowering of the allowable speed for automobiles to a walking pace. In fact, however, this equal status was not established in such areas. Nearly forgotten in the planning activities was the unarguable fact of the material power and great weight of the automobile.

Automobiles park in any open space in the traffic-calmed zones, although this is actually not allowed. A sign on the door of a house located in a traffic-calmed zone in the city Hannoversch Münden reads "Please leave a space wide enough for a baby carriage in front of our door" and indicates the relative roles of cars and pedestrians in such areas. Is it really necessary to rebuild a city to restrict and restrain the use of cars?

To begin with, the debate was shaped by people's demands for safety (particularly for children) and for a shared urban life that is socially attractive. The approach of slowing down cars in all cases and forcing them out of residential areas as much as possible led, however, to an increasing adoption of a Charter of Athens approach in which bypass streets were built. It also led to the implementation of some of Sir Colin Buchanan's ideas of building urban expressways around the borders of exclusively residential areas. The fact that traffic is naturally limited in mixed urban areas where there is a vital combination of functions and where a range of social classes reside was lost as a critical point in these discussions.

If one looks now to see where the majority of measures to achieve traffic calming have actually been carried out, one finds that it is in urban areas where the upper classes live. This supports the trend to create "purely residential areas", a feature of a functionalistic approach to urban planning. At the same time, the alternatively orientated action groups did not have effective arguments against newly constructed "bypass streets", as these had been promised as a means of keeping traffic out of residential areas. Since the beginning of the 1990s, large parts of the new street construction in Germany have been justified as a means of relieving and "calming" other areas. A broader approach of generally slowing down automobile traffic has been pursued only on a piecemeal basis. This has resulted in a growing tendency to sacrifice the objective of achieving equal status for all participants (pedestrians, bicyclists, car drivers) in the traffic mix. This occurred even though relevant expert assessments as well as practical examples from other international locations (the city of Graz in Austria, for example) have shown that a general reduction of speed limits is entirely possible and is very effective in promoting transport safety.

Some other counterexamples that demonstrate that different solutions are also feasible in Germany are worthy of mention. These include mixed areas (for example, Berlin-Moabit) where the existing street layout has been retained and the implementation of minor physical changes at the intersections has resulted in a successful reduction of speeds in automobile traffic. Likewise, the efforts undertaken under Transport Minister Christoph Zöpel in North Rhine-Westphalia of improving the living surroundings have achieved significant decreases in automobile speeds and a general gain in urban quality of life in mixed areas close to city centres. Also noteworthy are examples of larger areas with reduced speeds in Germany such as the Ruhr region cities of Dortmund and Bochum, which also instituted these measures at the initiative of Christoph Zöpel's ministry of transport and urban planning.[56]

More generally in Germany, however, it has been the case that the wave of "traffic calming" has in many cases destroyed the classic street configuration in its efforts to slow down cars, and at the same time has served as a justification for the construction of more and more ring roads and bypass streets. This in turn has led to a breaking up of city areas into ever smaller islands of urban settlement, isolated among a growing complex of expressways and bypasses. A further effect of these developments through the 1980s and 90s has been that urban fringe areas are nearly inaccessible for pedestrians trying to reach them from the city centre, owing to the multitude of uncrossable bypass roads.

A perfidious logic was employed in support of this approach and it had the additional unpleasant effect of causing the new bypass roads to be built in exceedingly large dimensions and for high-speed travel. The transport planners in the authorities responsible for road construction declared that the diversion of traffic away from urban and residential streets could only be successful if the bypass roads allowed for high-speed travel, thus "pulling" traffic away from the built-up urban areas. If one has taken on the premises of the Charter of Athens and the subsequent theories of Hans Bernhard Reichow and Sir Colin Buchanan, there is simply no other possibility than continually increasing the space devoted to streets to give traffic more space and reinforce the division of functions within the urban space. That the newly created traffic resulting from such expansion will create pressure for still more road construction has been conveniently forgotten in most instances. Only in isolated cases has it been possible for alternative transport planning to halt or reverse the upward spiral of traffic growth. These were instances in which urban planning and transport planning measures were coordinated and interlinked, making it possible to achieve real changes. The idea of a "city of short distances", which in effect would reduce traffic at the source by making it unnecessary for people to drive so much, was implemented far too little.

Outside of the cities, the successes of this alternative transport planning approach in Germany were limited. At the end of the 1980s, demands were made for the implementation of a speed limit on the autobahn and other roads outside the cities because of the environmental harm caused not only to people but also to green areas and forests in Germany. This led to a widely followed debate about the so-called "death of the forests". The forest in Germany had long been an idealised entity in the minds of the German bourgeoisie. Paintings of noble stags standing in stately configurations before towering spruce, fir, or oak trees could be found in many German living rooms at this time. Environmental organisations and committed transport engineers endeavoured to have a speed limit implemented with the argument that this would prevent the "dying of the forest".

The hope was that the classic German petit bourgeois could be mobilised with such an appeal. Looking back, this line of argument appears thoroughly ill advised. Driving more slowly on German autobahns needn't be a sacrifice made for the sake of the environment but rather could be promoted as an effective way to reduce stress and danger on the roads—as persons with experience of the highways in the USA or Switzerland, for example, could easily recognise. On the autobahns in Germany, the distance between cars travelling at very high speeds was becoming smaller and smaller, producing a situation similar to a professional car race. The more pertinent argument that this race, this daily competition that could easily end tragically in deadly accidents, had to be given up since it was nature, the forest, that "really" required that the speeds be lowered distorted the proper focus of the discussion.

In addition, technicians and engineers from the forestry industry and the automobile industry set about taking intensive measures to stop the increasing damage to German forests. The introduction of three-way catalytic converters in automobiles—marketed very adroitly to the public by German industry and the company BMW—together with extensive forestry initiatives (including slight changes in the statistical reporting detailing damage to the forests) created the impression that this small side issue could be resolved through technical measures. Some car drivers even took to driving with a bumper sticker that read "My Car Drives Without the Forest". This forest-protection line of argumentation has in fact impeded efforts to limit the speed on the autobahn network up to the present day. High-speed driving is seen as a value in itself, supporting among other things the export appeal of German automobiles; the effects on the environment are being limited by technology. The fact that virtually no time is saved through high-speed driving has been completely lost in the discussion. The higher likelihood of traffic jams caused by a higher number of automobile accidents at high speeds is also not being addressed.

In general, the development of automobile transport in Germany continues to follow the logic of an industrialised society. The central issue is to generate as much time saving as possible—whether real or only apparent. The idea persists that auto-bahn connections produce economic advantages for people and for regions. There is hardly any serious discussion of the fact that it has never been possible to prove that gains can be achieved in regional development or land-use planning through high-speed automobile travel.

The real effect of having an extended high-speed autobahn system is that regions and landscapes are becoming increasingly divided with a functional limi-tation of entire areas for specific purposes such as leisure or industry, and this topic is not a subject of discussion. Despite its initial successes, environmentally orientated transport planning has not managed to combine its ideas with an alter-native form of regional development or with new forms of urban planning apart from the few exceptions discussed above. A continuation of its early successes only seems possible if approaches such as those of Eckhard Kutter in academia and Christoph Zöpel in the political sphere are taken up, which can bring other forms of urbanity and urban planning into a vital relationship with an alternative form of transport planning.

The idea of growth imbedded in the logic of the Charter of Athens, the theories of Buchanan, and the "transport models" of the transport planners has continued to predominate, despite the emergence of an "alternative" movement.[57] The fact that this growth idea in the basic model for industrialisation will encounter drastic limits is not perceived. This will make some form of counter-development unavoidable, and in all probability this will come sooner than many imagine. However, for the moment in the decades since 1990 following the breakdown of the "socialist" system in Russia and Eastern Europe, critique of the existing arrangements in the west has been less focused and acute. The "growth" of the industrialised society has apparently been triumphant. This has led to a phase in transport that can be usefully characterised as "postmodern",[58] which will be discussed in detail in the following chapter.

Desolate Locations or the Forgotten Basis of a Critique of Modernism

When criticism of modernism is made in the fields of architecture and public life, this is typically done on the basis of an outer appearance. Particularly in modern societies, which through today's communication systems are strongly orientated to images,[59] facades and external appearances are often more important than back-ground factors. Thus modern architecture is often criticised for being ugly on the basis of its outer appearance; in the German city of Frankfurt, for example, there is a broad movement to rebuild old half-timbered buildings which are seen as repre-senting the "good times of the past".

Would the inner city of Frankfurt really be more beautiful if half-timbered facades were put up in front of the buildings of the banks? The organisational forms of urban life criticised in this book, which degrade urban spaces into realms of tran-sit through ever-higher speeds of passage, the increasing functional specialisation within the city, and the loss of small-scale urban networks and organisational units are causes for the desolation that can so often be found in urban situations. A critique that addresses external appearances neglects these deeper-lying issues.

As already shown, the development of modern long-distance transport has a particularly degrading effect on the immediate surroundings of where people live. This not only involves direct negative effects such as noise or exhaust emissions coming from traffic; it also concerns the real spaces and areas available for communication as well as the physical orientation points for traditional rules that facilitate interaction and common life that are forced out of the urban context. As individual urban areas come to be limited to a single function, the diversity and multiplicity of possibilities that support a vital living situation and allow mutually beneficial social relations are lost.

In his book *Non-places*,[60] the French author Marc Augé impressively describes how it is that places are only interesting for people when they can establish a relationship to the location. Relations cannot be established on the basis of rules or instruction or through the placement of benches or fountains, etc. An effective relationship between people and a place only comes about when the everyday social activities of the people are combined with a given location. Theoretically this can also occur with places that are far away from the living place of individuals. But in actual fact, the daily activities of well over 90 percent of people even in industrialised countries are concentrated on their residential environment and its immediate vicinity.

Furthermore, it is typically the case that the large facilities in distant places, which have replaced facilities in the more immediate vicinity, almost must serve a larger catchment area. This has the effect that clear rules must be formulated for using such facilities as strangers from more distant places are not familiar with them. The larger the distance and the faster the means of transport, the more the related actions to the activity of travel have to be regulated by publicly displayed rules, directions, and stipulations. Marc Augé calls this "the invasion of space by text". The intervening space between the residence of a person and his destination becomes anonymous and hardly perceivable on this basis. At the end of his book, Augé points to the almost desperate attempts to make the intervening space visible to the travellers who are passing through it. On a flight to Saudi Arabia, for example, the stewardess instructed passengers that while flying through Saudi airspace no alcohol should be consumed.[61]

As mentioned earlier in this chapter, Philippe Rekacewicz used his lecture at the documenta XII to point out the increasingly restrictive rules regarding the use of space in airports. He explained how direct control of the movement of passengers through the airport is exercised to the extent that the passengers are led (like sheep) through the duty-free shopping areas of the airport. The available space, which is what first constitutes a place, is shrinking. The characteristics of "real space" include that it can be occupied independently and that it provides a multitude of possibilities on the basis of simple rules. Only spaces of this sort can become the location for stories and subjective events that can later be told to others. Places can only be perceived as such when they come to exist in personal narratives and interesting stories.[62]

This should not be understood as an effort to romanticise such matters. Real places are also sites of contention and conflict. The point is that the organisational forms of a modern, distance-intensive way of life restrict small-scale, self-determined behaviour. This effect cannot be ameliorated by networking through the Internet, or in regional networks. It is revealing that many Internet programmes are virtually organised like a city or a village to pretend that some small-scale connection is provided. Finally, however, they cannot offer this because the contacts found there have no physical spatial dimension.

What applies for spaces is also true for many products that are brought to people at high speed from ever more distant locations and then find use in daily life. The purchase of food from a region brings the purchaser into a relationship with the season, the regional planting times, and the resulting quality of the products—all aspects of a particular region. With products coming from the super-modern food industry that are globally available without interruption through the year and put together using components from different countries, it is often impossible to have any idea where they really come from.[63]

What many people take to be the anonymity of modern forms of social organisation does not necessarily have to do with the appearance of things but rather with the organisational forms themselves in modern cities and production activities. These forms need not remain as they are currently, even in a global economy. There are numerous indications that even according to the criteria of an economic comparison of regions (which in itself is not a true reflection of quality of life), regions that are organised with small-scale local connections and a wide range of locally provided functions (as in Switzerland, for example) have significant advantages.

Postmodern Transport Planning

Even in the field of architecture, it is problematic to set an exact date for the beginning of a postmodern period. Thus it seems almost presumptuous to speak of postmodern transport planning. Nonetheless, it is possible to discern the beginning of a new phase in transport planning that commenced at the end of the 1980s or the beginning of the 90s. In this phase (and not only in Germany), greater attention is being given to forms and particularly to the "design" of transport facilities. In practice it is also the case that cities and regions must cope with new "fashions". In the following, we will refer to this phase as "postmodern transport planning", especially since there are characteristic parallels to the postmodern development in architecture.

In the field of architecture, various authors using a definition formulated by Charles Jencks identify the beginning of the postmodern period with the demolition of the Pruitt-Igoe housing development project in St. Louis, Missouri in 1972.[64] In that year more than 2,000 low-income apartments in a complex designed in the classic modernist style by the architect Minoru Yamasaki were demolished; the complex had existed since 1951. The definition makes use of the term postmodern as an explicit contradiction of the modern period with a renunciation of its fundamental principles (strikingly realised in the demolition of a classic modernist showpiece).

Charles Jencks made an effort to salvage this central element of the postmodern in a 2004 work directed against the numerous critics of postmodern architecture.[65] As a line of defence, he ascribed postmodern works to Jane Jacobs and other critics of modern urban planning and architecture. Nonetheless, even Jencks could not avoid noticing that "postmodernity (the combination of commercial global culture and mass mediation by the inventions of the electronic age) has destroyed much local culture, aided massive fraud at the Enron[66] scale, amplified celebrity culture and turned *ersatz* into 'business as usual'."

In practice, the examples of postmodern architecture (which will not be examined in greater detail here as regards their form and specifically architectural aspects) do not display a thoroughgoing critique of modernism in their urban planning and transport organisational features. While Jencks cites Jane Jacobs as an instance of postmodern architecture, it must also be noted that she was particularly critical of the modernist tendency to destroy traditional urban street spaces as well as of modernist transport organisation. But in postmodern architecture and planning, many of the errors of modernism in these sectors are repeated and then almost even more brutally.

Many postmodern buildings are solitary entities that take no note of the street space in relation to the entry situations of the buildings. One cannot speak in such instances of any sort of reclaiming of neighbourhood relations through a connection to the street (as described so impressively by Jane Jacobs). With the exception of a few examples in the work of Rob Krier or Kisho Kurokawa, both of whom plan using smaller blocks divided by streets, it may be remarked that the normal forms of access and interconnection developed in the modern period have not been questioned in any basic way in the postmodern period. In particular, the small-scale relationship between the house and the street, which was examined in detail in the first chapter of this book, has received very little attention from postmodern architects.

A renaissance of small-block planning—as found in three examples in the International Building Exhibition project in Berlin—did not tend to deal with the surrounding street space. The interior of the blocks on the other hand was intensively developed as a sort of "common room" for the housing project. This reorientation, which involved an effective turnaround of entrances, common spaces, balconies, etc. to the interior of the block, was hardly addressed by the architects. The space surrounding the larger block was simply left to the transport planners.

Transport planning itself escaped a process of radical change as occurred at least on a symbolic level in architecture with the demolition of Pruitt–Igoe. Transport planning built streets according to guidelines and technical considerations as seen "through the window of the automobile". The streets were orientated to the continued growth of automobile transport. A critique of such transport coming from postmodern architects, an integral element of the modern period, is difficult to find even if one looks very closely. Thus it is certainly not incorrect to state that transport planning reacted with some delay to the emerging criticism of modernism. What we here have termed somewhat boldly postmodern transport planning was first to be found in practice after 1985. Even if some positive examples of postmodern transport planning renewal can be cited, more generally it must be concurred in agreement with Jenck's citation above that the efforts in transport planning to react to the fashions of postmodernism were essentially fraudulent. In practice, this involved the vain attempt to give beauty to mistakes through the invocation of lies.

What does a postmodern street look like? The attempts to make a space "pretty", which is by and large unusable for pedestrians owing to the noise and the exhaust and the presence of automobiles, take different forms depending on the street type. With urban expressways and main thoroughfares, few physically based attempts were made. Sometimes these streets were decked out with pretty names such as "parkway" or "boulevard"—which they are not and cannot be. Sometimes colour was used—coloured asphalt, red plastered bicycle paths or different patterns decorating the marginal areas of such streets which should make them more attractive. When traffic noise makes it impossible to converse at the edge of such a street, a pretty pattern on the pavement does little to change this.

Significantly more extensive design efforts which should make street networks "nice" are to be found in residential areas or pedestrian zones. The traffic-calming measures mentioned in the previous chapter brought numerous new elements into the street space, particularly in Germany and Holland, that should suggest an improved level of habitability or beauty. Benches were distributed along the street space, trees were planted in median strips, fountains were erected. Decorative pavement patterns also had a prominent role here; contests were announced by various localities and designs were submitted for award juries to assess looking down from above at models of the proposed designs.

That real-life pedestrians do not view the street from a bird's-eye perspective and rather would like to have a well-secured pavement, that they want to be able to cross adjacent ring roads at regular intervals—these were matters that received less attention. Instead much consideration was devoted to certain details. Many small traffic-calming bumps were incorporated into the streets, typically in places where there was no need to cross the street; on the other hand, the selection of materials used for these fixtures was excellent. In retrospect, the fact that traditional materials were exported from cities in East Germany to West Germany in the mid-1980s for use in traffic-calmed zones in the West to give them an "old-fashioned" look seems very strange. There would be no basis for objecting to reasonably placed traffic-calming bumps at carefully selected locations where a genuine need exists to cross the streets (at schools, for instance). But often these placement decisions had no relation whatsoever to the actual function of the elements for the traffic. Often it was in fact the intention of the planners to "confuse" car drivers and other users of the street through an entirely illogical distribution of such design elements, as this confusion was thought to increase the awareness of individuals involved in the traffic situation.

This is a theory that the Dutch planner Hans Monderman brought into European planning circles with the aim of achieving local reductions in automobile speed through such "confusion". Currently this approach is referred to in Germany with the fashionable English term "shared space".[67] In individual streets of the city, a "slow network" should be established in which people once again have precedence over automobiles. In such areas the entire street space should be equally usable for pedestrians, bicyclists, and car drivers. To make that clear to all concerned, such spaces are given a new appearance and design. The separation of different traffic areas and lanes is eliminated and all traffic signs are removed.[68]

This idea that confusion produces a higher level of safety may be effective when car drivers have driven for a longer period through straight, clearly defined street spaces and then are suddenly confronted with a strange-seeming street situation that is difficult to interpret, giving them a distinct impression that their surroundings have changed in some basic way. But how should this strategy work with the elderly who need to be able to use the streets with a high level of safety and without "entering into communication with the car drivers"? And how should it work with children who must first learn how streets function in general and whose understanding of such matters will certainly not be heightened by encountering this sort of confusion?[69]

The zenith of such design efforts are certainly to be found in the pedestrian areas of the cities. This is where trade and service businesses are concentrated with the aim of attaining the highest possible revenues in local commerce. This is therefore where everything should look particularly nice and an impression of comfortable urban life should be created. Typically this will include lighting fixtures, which after long discussions in municipal committees will be embellished with elaborate baroque or medieval or art deco flourishes; paving that (depending on the state of the municipal budget) will feature expensive imported materials that in any case can stand up to cleaning with "Kärcher" cleaning machines; benches and wastepaper receptacles in strange designs and in unlikely places—all this is standard equipment for a German pedestrian zone.

In 1977, Werner Durth criticised the "ambivalence of urbanity" that is created through such pedestrian areas. Looking at the example of the shopping street "Zeil" in Frankfurt, he declared: "By taking away the cars from the Zeil, its monofunctional quality is even more evident."[70] It is not only this monofunctional aspect and the attempts to compensate for a missing urbanity through diverse postmodern "events" that tend to make the pedestrian zones in such cities negative spaces. It is also and especially the fact that they are separated from the rest of the city by ring roads that are built to bring cars and their drivers to the car parks at the periphery of the zone. It is this mistaken organisation of urban transport (traceable to Sir Colin Buchanan's work, *Traffic in Towns*) that helps us understand why it is that pedestrian areas typically fail.

At a workshop in Kassel, a proposal by a student of Lucius Burckhardt, Martin Schmitz, was greeted with astonishment. He suggested that at certain points regular streets should be allowed to cross the pedestrian area with automobile traffic. He connected this with the proposal to make the ring roads surrounding the inner city more easily crossable for pedestrians. A new form of urbanity—which postmodernism struggles to achieve in pedestrian areas through "events" or beach volleyball matches or a special kind of lighting in the Christmas season—can in fact only be had when the people of the city have a real, physically realised connection to their inner city. Without another concept of transport and traffic design, all the beautification efforts (which in essence don't go much beyond the selection of different sorts of pavement stones) will achieve nothing.

The streets themselves also receive more and more elements in an effort to "design" them. Particularly conspicuous are the roundabouts, which in Europe were originally used principally in the UK and now are increasingly being constructed in Germany and Austria as well. This approach to handling traffic flow is not unquestioned. Pedestrians and bicyclists, for example, derive little or no benefit from roundabouts and are in fact directly disadvantaged by them.[71] The element in the centre of the roundabout is the "design" feature. A guideline of German transport planning instructs that an object of urban identity should be placed there to give the people something to relate to. As a result, strange, often highly provincial-seeming "artworks" appear on the roundabouts. This might be the city crest laid out in stones, or a miniature windmill, or an old boulder. These objects should do something like cementing local relations, while the streets themselves become simple places of passage. Everywhere one finds the same sort of artificiality whether in the pedestrian zones or at the roundabouts. Ultimately, these paving objects and the supposed symbols of identification are utterly exchangeable.

The automobile itself has also become an "event" in postmodern transport. In an expensively produced book-like tome from the Volkswagen company given to car buyers at the time of purchase, an effort is made to turn the automobile into a cultural object.[72]

At the production facility for the company's top-of-the-range cars in Dresden, one finds a sign that reads: "Here culture is being made. Before your eyes." These most expensive cars have to be "experienced";[73] the automobile is referred to as a "Lebensraum" (living space).[74] A high point of cultural experience with the automobile is apparently a visit to the so-called "Autostadt" in the VW company town of Wolfsburg. It is indeed strange that an artificial location, which Volkswagen uses to pay homage to its products, is referred to as a "Stadt" or city. As the promotion literature declares: "Here a city visit of a special sort is waiting for you. Under the motto, 'People, Cars and What Moves Them', the Autostadt illuminates one of the central themes of our life—mobility with the help of exhibits, artworks, installations and a wide range of events."[75]

Of course, in the "Autostadt" one goes on foot. In the entire volume from VW, there is little or nothing to be found about the negative effects of automobiles; emergency services take care of such matters as traffic jams or accidents. The automobile itself becomes a spectacle; the image shown here has nothing to do with matters of daily use. The concept of mobility has gained a sort of trendiness, whereby it is not in the least clear what it really means. However, through its association with terms like culture, experience, entertainment, or even "a drive in the country", it seems to acquire ecological characteristics.

Of course, the automobile is not the only product that is elaborately presented. The same is true of most any other product group as well, particularly the transport that is connected with them. The global division of labour and the low price for transport, which do not reflect the true costs and consequences for the users of such services, are also leading to more and more intensive and far-reaching transport processes in the freight sector. The strawberry yoghurt described by Stefanie Böge in 1992, which consisted of ingredients from all over Europe, meanwhile belongs to the past.

A Swiss pupil recently wrote in his A-level qualifying exam about a Greek yoghurt that appeared in East Germany in a supermarket. It is not presumptuous to assume that industrially prepared foods typically have places of origin that go far beyond the continent where the final processing facility is located. The identification by means of its place of origin is thus becoming increasingly obsolete. Today before it is sold, an entirely normal pair of trousers will be transported over various continents. The material comes from one country, the cutting is done in another, sewing takes place someplace entirely different, buttons and the company tag come from still another place until such a product acquires its brand name and the stamp "Made in Germany", and then is sent to the shop by the seller. Against this background, consumers orient themselves increasingly on the basis of global brands which seem to promise them some sort of security.

But this is often nothing but a sort of fraud. Corporations such as the Italian company Benetton are in fact nothing other than global logistic concerns. Such a company purchases the products it will later sell on the global market and then markets them under its brand with a flashy advertising campaign without having anything further to do with the products. With foodstuffs, an attempt is typically made to establish a relationship to a concrete space – if only on an imaginary basis. With meat products, a picture of a traditional-looking farm often appears on the packaging; with milk products one sees cows in a mountain meadow. The fact that meat ordinarily comes from mass-production Belgian butcheries and is driven over the Alps to Italy to then be sold in Germany as classic Italian prosciutto is, of course, not presented on the packaging. A picture of a mass-production Belgian slaughterhouse or a lorry on the highway would be more appropriate images to put on the packaging to provide information about the origin of the product.

Even though numerous large corporations make the claim today that they produce on a green and sustainable basis, the reality of global production, particularly as regards transport factors, looks quite different. The environmental damage caused by production-based transport continues to grow while postmodern transport planning does all it can to conceal this damage and deceive consumers. In this respect, we find ourselves again with Jencks and his admission regarding the "massive fraud" of postmodernism. The field of transport planning makes its own contribution to this deception and at the same time has much less of a positive nature to offer than do postmodern architects. The following chapter therefore deals with the question of how an alternative form of transport planning could react to this development and which steps are still available to be taken.

The Locality in Global Competition or the City as a Point in a Transport Network

In the context of the development of the postmodern city that defines itself through images and outwardly projected characteristics, the view of transport and the role of transport networks continue to change. In the modern city, distance and the reachability of faraway points has gained more and more significance. This orientation is now approaching a new pinnacle. Small-scale connections within a locality have become fully irrelevant in the international and now global competition among locations. For most of the politicians and influential managers of urban locations, the only relevant factor is a city's role in the global transport network.[76]

The public image of a city is increasingly based on how easily it can be reached from other places. It has become more important that global centres such as New York or Beijing can be reached in a short flying time from an airport in Europe than whether one can get from a particular airport into the city proper in a reasonable period of time. A pertinent example of this attitude, which has become more and more entrenched since the 1980s, is provided in the remarks of the mayor of the small city of Calden located in the German state Hesse. At a university seminar, he reported his experiences dealing with the provincial city's plans to expand its airport. "I was in New York," he recounted. "In the Chamber of Commerce there they didn't know anything about Calden. But they told us, if we had an airport that was connected to the global air travel network then they would know us." The mayor looked at his audience with the assumption that this was a telling argument. When he was asked how one would reach the new global airport planned in his small city from Kassel, the closest city and business centre of any consequence that the airport would principally serve, this seemed of far less relevance to him. In fact, the regional accessibility of this newly expanded airport (the sense of which is certainly a matter of debate) has not in the least been considered. From Kassel, one can reach the airport in Paderborn just as quickly as the new facility in Calden. Calden's connection to the public transport network is, to put it mildly, dismal.

But this is not the issue here. What has become of consequence is that the city or some location wishes to become a special point on a fictive map of the world without any interest remaining for the inner situation in the city or the broader vicinity of the surrounding region. The characteristics of the inner connections and connectivity of a location, the communication and the creativity existing between the persons living there, lose all relevance. What is important instead is that the place is located on a transport connection between supposedly significant destinations bearing big names.

With the exceedingly costly and elaborate German railroad station project "Stuttgart 21", it was emphasised from the commencement of the planning in the 1980s and 90s that it was important that Stuttgart is now located on the "Paris-Budapest axis" and therefore is positioned to play a more important global role. It was not until intensive discussions in 2010 with protesting citizens in the planning process seeking a compromise for the station development that the Deutsche Bahn and the planning authorities admitted that this argument had no real significance, because almost no one travelled from Paris to Budapest. The accessibility of Paris or Budapest from Stuttgart was merely a new argument in line with contemporary marketing that the city would then have used without further inquiry. Stuttgart, an important city, because it lies on the axis between Paris and Budapest—this in probability would have been the message.

The definition of places in terms of the large facilities that are located there, through advertising slogans directed to an audience outside the place itself, becomes the driving argument in planning discussions rather than what the city in fact has to offer. In the planning of long-distance highways in Germany and in the rest of Europe, this type of argumentation is used in a manner that residents living along such a route have little recourse against. The new autobahn closes the gap between Amsterdam and Kiev; this is the argument for a motorway that runs close to the German city of Kassel towards the even smaller municipality of Eisenach. What does that mean for the residents who live along this stretch who don't wish to deal with the noise of the roadway on a daily basis?

It is only late in the process that citizens on site where such large-scale projects[77] are constructed realise that they no longer play a significant role. Their everyday life does not play out between New York and Madrid. A lorry driving past their homes does not necessarily bring growth and innovation to their region. It becomes increasingly clear that these distant connections do not deliver benefits but rather drawbacks through the increasingly global production of anonymous products. This is the point at which the on-site living conditions of people and the best way of handling this specific here-and-now situation again become the focus of interest, if only through these people's own self-interest and initiative.

Nonetheless, the idea persists that a location's easy accessibility from distant locations is far more important than the inner organisation and communication within a city itself. The notion that a city is simply a point that only has to be marketed in the right way remains central in postmodern thinking, and it will take a long time for this distorted view to vanish from the contemporary mind.

Notes

1 A stronger emphasis on the material aspects of spatial organisation was proposed in 1983 by Hans Linde in his book *Sachdominanz in Sozialstrukturen* (Technical Dominance in Social Structures).
2 See Lefèbvre, H. 2005, particularly chapter 2 in which Lefèbvre derives the concept of social space making reference to Hegel, Marx, and Engels and illustrates the concept in connection with urban spaces and regions such as Venice and Tuscany.

3 The urban sociologist Thomas Krämer-Badoni, for example, rejects the idea that the concept of social space could be useful (see Krämer-Badoni 2003). Later, however, he qualified this rejection when he proposed a method for determining the effect of spatial elements on social factors, making reference to the Swiss sociologist Stichweh.

4 Stichweh, R. 2003, pp. 93–102.

5 Cf. Hägerstrand, T. 1970.

6 Ibid., in particular pp. 14 ff.

7 See Hägerstrand, T.: "Today differences between groups within the same area and differences between areas can be very great", 1970, p. 13.

8 See Illich, I. 1975, p. 28.

9 Interesting against this background is a hypothetical model of unlimited and cost-free ultra-high-speed locomotion for all persons, i.e. the absence of any distance-based resistance. Torsten Hägerstrand discussed this example at a conference in France in 1982 at which the author was present. Hägerstrand depicted this as a horrible situation in which the subject could be in all places but would be at home nowhere; in effect, mankind would lose an effective relation to space.

10 Despite these controls and regulations, the automobile is still the most dangerous technical product besides weapons of war that has shaped the twentieth century. By far the highest number of unnatural deaths are attributed to the automobile.

11 See Davis, M. 2007, p. 11. Davis explains that car bombs are astoundingly powerful and destructive camouflaged weapons as such vehicles can effectively transport large explosive payloads. A normal family car can transport a 500-kg bomb without difficulty.

12 Reinier Zwitsersloot, the chairman of the board of the company Wintershall in Kassel, demanded in 2008 for example that the nearby airport Kassel-Calden be expanded as he could not be expected to make a stopover in Italy on his way to Libya using the small private jet that Kassel-Calden could accommodate at that time. In the meantime, the airport has been expanded, if not only for Mr Zwitsersloot. For passengers of his sort, the controls at the airport are, of course, significantly faster.

13 See Beck, Ulrich 2009, pp. 32–33. Beck argues that the globally imagined or indeed real risks are an essential justification for the existence of global coordination groups such as the "G20". Plans to "save the world" seem to become necessary due to the ever shrinking degree of influence over distant matters to avoid global risks. Considerable problems of democratic legitimation arise from this situation – and not only in connection with the "G20" – to make the point together with Beck in a very understated manner.

14 See Isbary, G. 1965.

15 See Schekahn, A. 1998, p. 170.

16 See Fahlbusch, M. 2003, p. 569.

17 The word "axis" came to prominence in the 1930s. Mussolini spoke in 1936 of the Berlin-Rome axis, which eventually gave rise to the designation "Axis" to describe the principal partners Germany, Italy, and Japan in their conflict with the Allies in the Second World War.

18 See Bongards, M. G. 2004, p. 97.

19 See van Laak, D. 2005, pp. 92 ff.; the conclusion (from p. 185) is also interesting.

20 Whereby this aspect of course remains a part of such large technical projects. See Ullrich, O. 1977, pp. 314 ff, where Ullrich explicitly deals with large transport projects such as railway lines or airports.

21 See, for example, Schröteler von Brand, H. 2008, p. 152 f.

22 Only 5 km of the project were realised due to cost reasons.

23 See Chambless, E. 2009 (based on the original of 1910).

24 Also playing a role here, in addition to the land prices, were health aspects or the well-known idea of the good life in a "garden city" in accordance with the model of the planner E. Howard.

25 See here and in the following Divall, C. and Bond, W. (eds.) 2003.

26 See Marinetti, F. T. 1909, or the pictures of Antonio Sant'Elia.

27 Cf. Joachimsthaler, A. 1999.
28 Of course, the role models also changed with the end of the war. Prior to the German defeat it was Adolf Hitler with his gargantuan ideas that served as the rationale for such plans. After the war it was the role model of the victors, the Allies. Their industrial production of vehicles, weapons, and other modern military logistic materials were invoked when the development of new large-scale technically orientated industries and a modern transport network was discussed.
29 A factory for the "Kraft durch Freude" (KdF—strength through joy) automobile based on the plans of a company with the name "Gezuvor" was built here in 1938 on the direct orders of Hitler. The place was called "Stadt des KdF—Wagens bei Fallersleben". It is interesting that Ferdinand Porsche took ideas for the production of the KdF automobile from the USA and recruited engineers of German origin who had emigrated there. Elements of mass production were thus certainly to be found in fascism and were represented in the modernisation wing of the Nazi Party. Large numbers of forced labourers (including some from Italy) built the factory and the first automobiles. Torture and death were part of the daily routine. (On this subject, see Bermani, C.; Bologna, S.; Mantelli, B. 1997, pp. 94–97.) The name "Wolfsburg" was adopted after the Second World War and refers to a nearby castle of that name.
30 That for a long time little or nothing was said about the brutal manner in which these factories were erected, often with the use of forced labour, is also worthy of note.
31 See Sieverts, T. 1997.
32 Spiegel, E. 1974, p. 98.
33 On this point see Gassner, E. 1974, p. 323.
34 Ibid., p. 324.
35 See Isbary, G. 1965, p. 10.
36 Ibid., p. 4.
37 Ibid., p. 3.
38 Alexander von Papp recommends, for example, "that in areas primarily intended for agricultural production and ecological function a certain depopulation effort could be positively supported", 1976, p. 75.
39 See Traube, K. 1983 and Ullrich, O. 1977.
40 This is particularly evident with food production (see here, for example, Böge, S. 2003).
41 It is not our intention to discuss here whether, where, and to what degree large-sized facilities and extreme division of labour make sense, i.e. what the "optimal" size of a given facility should be. This is a complex problem that must be evaluated on a case-by-case basis depending on the type of facility or production unit. It is indisputable, however, that the global division of labour and the shipment of essential similar foodstuffs from one continent to another have reached a level that makes no sense. The dependence on transport and petroleum is disastrous; the compulsion to grow in size and distance finds its limit in the ability to provide energy for such activities. See Altvater, E. 2006, p. 107 f.
42 See here and in the following: Der Spiegel (issue no. 34) 1963, pp. 24–34.
43 Der Spiegel (issue no. 34) 1963, p. 27.
44 Der Spiegel (issue no. 34) 1963, p. 24.
45 Transport Minister Georg Leber was actually the pioneering advocate of today's lorry toll system that was introduced under a Red-Green government in January 2005. This system incidentally has had nearly as little success as Leber's plan in reducing lorry traffic. Due to the influence of the trucking lobby, there has been almost no increase in the costs for lorry transport companies.
46 Der Spiegel (issue no. 34) 1963, p. 31.
47 Kutter, E. 1975.
48 Cf. Thaler A.; Winkler M. 2005, pp. 117–121.
49 See Mitscherlich, A. 1969 (first edition 1965).
50 Ibid., p. 40 f.
51 Ibid., p. 92.

52 The lord mayor of Munich Jochen Vogel also had an important influence with his early formulation of a critique of the automobile.

53 See "Bürgerinitiative Westtangente" (editor) 1976.

54 See Holzapfel, H.; Traube, K.; Ulrich, O. 1985.

55 Ibid.

56 See Zöpel, C. 2008.

57 See here and in the following Thaler, A.; Winkler, M. 2005, pp. 117–121.

58 The term "postmodern" was used much earlier in urban planning and architecture than in transport planning.

59 See Pörksen, U. 1997, p. 14 ff.

60 See Augé, M. 1995.

61 Ibid.

62 See Burckhardt, L. 2006, p. 114 ff.

63 See Böge, S. 1993, pp. 132–159.

64 The demolition of Pruitt-Igoe as the starting point of postmodernism was defined by Charles Jencks. See Jencks, C. 1977, p. 9.

65 See Jencks, C. 2004, pp. 12–31.

66 Enron was an American energy company that made huge profits through massive accounting fraud over a long period of time and then went bankrupt in 2001.

67 See Keuning Instituut, Senza Communicatie 2005.

68 Monderman also makes note of the fact that this "slow network" can only function when there is also a "fast network" where the general rules of automobile traffic apply, because otherwise the "slow network" would not be accepted by car drivers.

69 See Westermann, A. 2000, p. 7 f.

70 See Durth, W. 1977, p. 140 ff.

71 See Holzapfel, H. 2010, pp. 2–5.

72 See Volkswagen AG (publisher), undated.

73 Ibid., p. 40 ff.

74 Ibid., p. 62 f.

75 Ibid., p. 30 f.

76 On the global location competition, see also Twickel, C. 2010, p. 27.

77 On the subject of largeness in postmodernism, see also Kaltenbrunner, R. 2010.

5

BRIDGES IN THE ARCHIPELAGO

Creating New Networks

The city has always been a complex nexus of a multitude of relationships; in the direct vicinity of the flats and houses of the people, these relationships have come to be severely restricted in the course of recent history. When calls are made for the city to assume a role as "the site of production for the new" in society or as "the platform of exchange", a strengthening of these inner networks is required. Places have increasingly become like archipelagos,[1] groups of small, even tiny islands, between which (to continue the metaphor) the automobile traffic has assumed the role of water separating the pieces of landed settlement.

A new beginning must be made with the street. As the basis of the local exchange of information, the site for encounters among people, and a place where a life in common can unfold, the street is extremely important (see Chapter 3, Figure 3.3). The street will become still more important because the phase of what the sociologists refer to as the Fordistic production society, with its fixation on the output of high numbers and large volumes of goods, will give way to a new order requiring new ideas, visions, and changes. An intellectual renewal of this sort is not to be had without informal meetings and direct encounters between conflicting elements. A city can only spawn such ideas, such "newness", when it not only represents an instance of concentrated and compacted difference[2] but also has a means of dealing with this difference through a process of interaction leading to a reasonable future.

Exchange via electronic communication technology, which often takes place in the form of a "virtual city", cannot replace this process.[3] What does this mean? Urbanity has nothing to do with skyscrapers, with conglomerations of cultural attractions, with staged events.[4] The street must be reclaimed as a place of communication through direct contact. Classic zoning, simple rules, and easy street crossing are an initial basis for this. The current nonsense of "shared-space" methods popular in alternative circles clearly degrades the conditions of communication. Classic, long-proven models as found, for example, in the popular Gründerzeit districts of German cities demonstrate that such an approach works. The networks of streets and bicycle and footpaths have not received sufficient attention in many urban planning situations or have been left exclusively to transport planners who only think of optimising conditions for cars. In this book we have seen from the beginning that just as mixed use and density of population are integral to successful urbanity, so too is the small-scale organisation of the street network.

What should happen with the cars? We have seen that in densely settled, closely organised urban neighbourhoods, car-based transport continues to take place. In such instances, however, it is small-scale transport that predominates rather than long-distance travel. In the article "How Urban Planning Generates Car Traffic" ("Das Wohnen macht den Verkehr"), the Austrian Transport Club shows how a well-functioning urban area in effect "automatically" has 30 percent less automobile traffic. This requires no limitations, artificial measures, or reconstruction of streets.

Reduction of the speed limit for cars to 30 kilometres per hour (which in these areas in any case would be difficult to exceed), the "reopening" of intersections (which had been closed in connection with ill-advised traffic management concepts) and the regular placement of pedestrian crosswalks are collectively fully sufficient to achieve this effect. A person who is sitting at the side of the street, communicating with his or her neighbour, is not sitting in an automobile driving around looking for something far away.

Seeking distant places will without doubt become more expensive in the coming years. New automobile technologies, electric-powered automobiles, and futuristic vehicles of other sorts will have one distinguishing feature for certain: they will be more expensive than today. Well-functioning, small-scale communication for "all" will therefore also have the benefit of providing more social equality. This, however, will only be the case when we have cities for all. Lucius Burckhardt, who has already been cited frequently in this book, pointed out in the days of his famous "Lehrcanapé" in Zurich that architects and planners should not only build structures but also continually question for whom they are building them. The vast majority of the population spends a large part of the day in the vicinity of where they reside and will continue to do so in the future. Urban planning, architecture, and transport planning must again take these people into account.

But it remains important to continue to ensure the possibility of diversity. This diversity has not only been removed from cities with the decline of mixed-use urban planning; there is also a threat of increased division within cities between different population groups, a trend that already exists in many places. The strengthening of small-scale immediate networks should not only make connections but also bring together what is unwished with what is wished. Functionalistic Fordist automobile networks totally confound such an approach of forging connections between highly different elements in the city. What can be done in an immediate way to counter this?

Step by step, the chopping up of cities with expressway systems and bypass roads must be overcome. Any well-designed crossing of a city expressway should be more important to a good city planner than a new high-speed connection to Rome or Brussels. Pedestrians should not only be found in the zones that are especially reserved for them. The zones should perhaps not be for the pedestrians alone but rather form another functional archipelago island in the city. Islands must be gradually built up through effective networking between the islets, which then can be connected with one another through lines of communication and exchange.[5] The city must make it possible for all its participants and inhabitants to actively take part and exchange with one another. This also means that special privileges, the exclusion of certain persons or groups, or the payment of fees for the use of public spaces are not effective measures; rather they are precisely the opposite, producing only an appearance of urbanity.[6]

The desire of transport planners to provide something like peace and quiet through the unending creation of new diversions and displacements of traffic to "somewhere else", so that "here" in front of one's own house it is possible to comfortably cross the street, has proved to be a vain illusion. Displacements and diversions simply create new separations in the city and, continuing the image we have used before, enlarge the expanses of water between the islands of the archipelago. In the preceding text it has been clearly shown that since the "bypass road" was invented in the 1920s, it has only served as a justification for a development that in principle serves the further expansion of automobile use.

Public transport in the cities can and should support small-scale networking within and between neighbourhoods. Many cities in Europe as well as many new urban localities in the Third World have public transport systems in which the distances between the stops are too large; this makes for bad accessibility in the immediate vicinity. Attention in such situations is often focused on long-distance trains and high-speed routes; the significance of such systems is often exaggerated in comparison to the development of a local tram system or the establishment of an additional stop on an existing rail line.[7]

A city with a dynamic future must be a city that is creating new possibilities. No one can be told which of these possibilities he or she should take up. The process of the development of urban communication networks from 1900 to the present described in this book unfortunately shows nothing other than the reduction of the range of choice for people in this historical period. Instead of the people being offered a growing multitude of possibilities, the where and how of their exchange and movement in the urban context have been more and more narrowly prescribed (in the pedestrian zone, for example). The faster the technology and the higher the top speed of a transport system, the more precisely they determine the behaviour of their users as well as the behaviour of those who do not use them at all.

Cities with well-functioning internal networks will therefore once again become places of lower speeds. The movement of "slow cities" that began in Italy is certainly a step in the right direction. Distant locations can continue to be reachable in such a situation. But the process of recent decades that has been based on a one-sided preference for the accessibility of distant destinations must come to an end; it must be brought to a level that allows for and gives precedence to a viable common life on the streets and in the neighbourhoods that directly surround us.[8]

Notes

1 According to the nineteenth edition of the German Brockhaus Encyclopedia, an archipelago is a group of islands (1987, p. 81). The term goes back to the archipelago existing between Greece and Asia Minor consisting of small and even tiny islands between which large areas of water are found. This image is highly reminiscent of the contemporary city, if one imagines the water as the traffic areas devoted to automobiles. In all probability, the sea of the classic Greek archipelago was easier to cross than the traffic masses in today's cities.
2 See Twickel, C. 2010, p. 20.
3 See, for example, Juli Zeh: "Stop," I interrupt F. "Don't tell me anything about the advent of post-capitalism coming through Internet communication. I'll believe that when the first open-source bakery has opened in my neighbourhood." Zeh, J. 2010, p. 24.
4 See here also Feldtkeller, A. 1994, p. 168. Feldtkeller, however, neglects the street as the direct surrounding of the place of residence in his remarks.
5 See also Feldtkeller, A. 1994, p. 168.
6 See Holzapfel, H. 2010.
7 In Germany this is one of the main reasons why large train station projects or new high-speed trains are increasingly greeted with scepticism by the public. See, for example, the protests against the train station project, Stuttgart 21.
8 Cf. Kenworthy, J.; Newman, P. 1999 and 2006.

6

WHAT ARE EXAMPLES OF NEW TRANSPORT PLANNING IN GERMANY AND IN EUROPE AS A WHOLE?

Some of the new perspectives regarding transport and urbanism presented in this book are shared by transport specialists in Germany and Europe, at least at a formal level; others, of course, are not. It is, however, the political reality that lags furthest behind the various positions discussed and advocated in scholarly circles. Nonetheless, in real transport practice in Germany changes are occurring, especially in the everyday behaviour of ordinary people. These changes are remarkable, occurring as they do in the country where the automobile was first invented and in which there still remains no speed limit on major motorways, and they are also noteworthy when compared with developments in other countries. They are indicative of the growing reach of new transport perspectives in Germany, which are also influencing other states and the situation in Europe in general.

The basic starting point of all these new perspectives is a slowly emerging change in how people regard the automobile and deal with it. For example, twenty years ago it was an established rite of passage for nearly all young people to acquire a driving license as early as legally possible on their eighteenth birthday and thus become able to make use of the automobile. Today, up to 20 percent of the students beginning their studies at the University of Kassel are not in possession of a driving license.[1]

Such a "life without the car" is becoming increasingly possible through improvements in public transport not only in the cities but also in suburban areas around cities throughout Europe.[2] A further aspect of this trend (particularly for students) is the very favourable fare plans available for the use of trams and buses.

It isn't just young people who are adopting different driving practices. The general rates of growth for using public transport in urban areas is higher than the growth rates of automobile traffic.[3] Indeed, an intensive discussion (the so-called "peak car debate") is underway in expert circles in transport policy in Europe regarding the question of whether growth in private car use will in fact continue in the coming years. At the same time, however, the centralisation of industrial facilities, educational institutions, hospitals, and other services essential for everyday life continues apace. The division of production labour continues to increase in Europe and worldwide, promoted by an intensive subsidisation of freight transport and long-distance transport in general. This takes manifold forms: trucks that pay for only a fraction of the wear and damage they cause on roadways; airplanes and ships that pay virtually no taxes and further subsidies that purportedly sustain the economies of Europe. These are consequences of the central error identified and analysed in this book—namely, the belief that the support of transport to distant destinations improves living conditions in Europe.

As a result, the national and global division of labour is intensified and reinforced, which in turn generates further increases in the volume of transport. Even the welcome growth figures for public transport in Germany and Europe can therefore not be viewed entirely positively. If the volume of public-transport trips is only increasing because people cannot organise their daily lives without travelling more, this is not a favourable development.

Europe can and must be a model for an emerging form of mobility that can be transferred to the rest of the world without causing damage. This will include cities where automobiles are hardly used, erstwhile "transport corridors" where people can once again live and work, and societies where friendships and personal relations are not only carried out through virtual means. The city's diversity and its capacity to integrate, its inclusion of disadvantaged groups and assimilation of foreign elements—all these factors demand genuinely urban conditions.[4] The theories that attribute creativity to the city may in certain respects be exaggerated and be shaped by an unreflective concept of growth; nonetheless, it is indisputable that the contradictions and confrontations that are integral to the urban setting are a key prerequisite for the development of new ideas.

While political institutions and globally orientated industries continue to promote the development of long-distance transport, people in many places in Europe have come to another decision. Dedicated paths for pedestrians and bicycles are on the increase in cities; the public spaces and street cafés even in the northern cities of Germany and Europe are more and more heavily frequented. Conducting everyday business on foot and particularly by bicycle has been steadily increasing in Germany since approximately 2002—following years of decline. Individual transport in motorised vehicles, on the other hand, is no longer increasing or is even falling in the statistics. These figures reflect average values which also include rural settlements.

In cities with well-maintained historical transport facilities for pedestrians or in newly developed settlements that have been planned on a small-scale basis with mixed-use neighbourhoods, the diminishing role of the automobile is even more evident. The so-called "French Quarter" in Tübingen is a well-known example. Only 10 percent of individual trips from home are conducted there with the automobile; 47 percent are done with the bicycle, 31 percent on foot, and 13 percent by public bus.[5] These are values that point to a form of development that is sustainable on a long-term basis. In fact, the city of Tübingen has the current goal of improving these values and cutting CO_2 emissions by a further 50 percent.

In Europe, the locations that are full of automobiles such as the German cities of Stuttgart, Hamburg, or Dortmund are no longer admired; instead, public admiration is directed towards urban locations such as Copenhagen in Denmark or Freiburg and Tübingen in Germany that can serve as a model for future development. Even in a major metropolis like Paris, car-free days on the banks of the Seine are a great success.

The transformation of our cities can occur on a decentralised basis, and indeed this is what is happening—a regaining of the streets and public spaces of the cities as a place for people to lead their lives (rather than for cars to drive about), one neighbourhood at a time. Large areas in the cities could soon function successfully without automobiles. Movements such as the "slow city" initiative (cittaslow), which started in Italy and is now internationally active, are taking up these ideas and gaining more and more support. Each new pedestrian crossing a street, each tree growing where a car was once parked, each place where children can once again play safely on a city street is important – more important to be sure than any new air connection from New York to Rome or elsewhere.

Notes

1 This was found in regular surveys at first-semester events for students at Kassel University conducted since 1995. The causes of young people's changing behaviour in connection with the automobile are currently being researched. The causes and permanence of the phenomenon are under discussion and not yet entirely clarified. See in this connection, Bock, B.; Deibel, I.; Schönduwe, R.: Alles wie immer, nur irgendwie anders? Trends und Thesen zu veränderten Mobilitätsmustern junger Menschen (Everything as always, but somehow different? Trends and theses regarding changing patterns of mobility among young people). In: InnoZ-Baustein 10, Berlin 2012.
2 Numerous improvements have been achieved in recent years, particularly with rail transport through the development of local transport systems, for example with so-called tram-train systems in Nordhessen in Germany as well as in various regions in France.
3 See, for example, the figures of the Verband Deutscher Verkehrsunternehmen (VDV— Association of German Public Transport Companies) for the year 2012, in particular for metropolitan centres.
4 See, for example, Saunders, D.: Arrival City—How the Largest Migration in History Is Reshaping Our World, London 2011.
5 These figures were obtained in a study in 2011 by Stefan Walter of the Institute for Street and Transport Studies at Graz University of Technology (TU Graz).

BIBLIOGRAPHY

Ahrens, Gerd-Axel; Hubrich, Stefan; Ließke, Frank; Wittwer, Rico: Zuwachs des städtischen Autoverkehrs gestoppt!? In: Straßenverkehrstechnik, issue 12, 2010, pp. 769–777.

Alexander, Christopher: A city is not a tree. Architectural Forum 122 April 1965, no. 1, no. 2. Reprinted in: Design after Modernism, edited by John Thackara, Thames and Hudson, London 1988; see also in: Human Identity in the Urban Environment, edited by G. Bell and J. Tyrwhitt, Penguin 1992.

Altvater, Elmar: Das Ende des Kapitalismus wie wir ihn kennen. Münster 2006.

Appleyard, Donald D.: Livable streets. Berkeley/Los Angeles 1981.

Aristoteles: Politik. Buch I und II, translated by Eckhard Schütrumpf. Berlin 1991.

Augé, Marc: Non-places. An introduction to supermodernity. London 1995.

Battis, Ulrich: Die Europäische Stadt – Auslaufmodell oder Kulturgut und Kernelement der Europäischen Union. Berlin 2008.

Bäuerle, Heidbert; Theiling, Christoph: Plätze in Bremen. Platz haben und Platz lassen. In: AG Freiraum und Vegetation (pub.); Bremer Reihen. Notizbuch 44 der Kasseler Schule. Kassel 1996.Beck, Ulrich: Weltinnenpolitik. In: Frankfurter Rundschau, 4 October 2009.

Benevolo, Leonardo: Die Geschichte der Stadt. Frankfurt/New York 1983.

Bermani, Cesare; Bologna, Sergio; Mantelli, Brunello: Proletarier der Achse. Berlin 1997.

Bernhardt, Katja: Hans Bernhard Reichows 'Gedanken zur städtebaulichen Entwicklung des Groß-Stettiner Raumes' (1940). Darstellung des Wirkens des Architekten in Stettin 1936 –1945 und Analyse der Schrift. Magisterarbeit (master's thesis) at the Humboldt-Universität Berlin. Berlin 2003.

Beyme, Klaus von; Durth, Werner; Gutschow, Niels (eds.): Neue Städte aus Ruinen, Deutscher Städtebau der Nachkriegszeit. München 1992.

Bock, Benno; Deibel, Inga; Schönduwe, Robert: Alles wie immer, nur irgendwie anders? Trends und Thesen zu veränderten Mobilitätsmustern junger Menschen. In: Innovationszentrum für Mobilität und gesellschaftlichen Wandel (pub.); InnoZ-Baustein 10, Berlin 2012.

Bodenschatz, Harald: Europäische Stadt, Zwischenstadt und New Urbanism. In: PlanerIn 3/2001.

Böge, Stefanie: Erfassung und Bewertung von Transportvorgängen: Die produktbezogene Transportkettenanalyse. In: Dieter Läpple (ed.); Güterverkehr, Logistik und Umwelt, Analysen und Konzepte zum interregionalen und städtischen Verkehr. Berlin 1993.

Böge, Stefanie: Äpfel. Vom Paradies bis zur Verführung im Supermarkt. Dortmund 2003.

Bongards, Martin Gerhard: Raumplanung als wissenschaftliche Disziplin im Nationalsozialismus. Marburg 2004.

Bourdieu, Pierre et al.: Der Einzige und sein Eigenheim. Extended new edition. Hamburg 2002.

Brockhaus Enzyklopädie, 19th edition. Gütersloh 1987.Burckhardt, Jacob: Das Geschichtswerk. Licensed edition. Frankfurt am Main 2007.

Burckhardt, Lucius: Bauen ein Prozess. Niederteufen 1968. In: Stadt-Landschaft 2030. Forschungsergebnisse TU Braunschweig. Braunschweig 2004.

Burckhardt, Lucius: Warum ist Landschaft schön? – Die Spaziergangswissenschaft. Berlin 2006.

Burckhardt, Lucius: Wer plant die Planung? In: Pehnt, Wolfgang; Die Stadt in der Bundesrepublik. Lebensbedingungen, Aufgaben, Planung. Stuttgart 1974.

Burckhardt, Lucius: Wer plant die Planung? Architektur, Politik und Mensch. Berlin 2004.

Bürgerinitiative Westtangente (ed.): Stadtautobahnbau – Ein Schwarzbuch zur Verkehrsplanung. Berlin 1976.

Chambless, Edgar: Roadtown. BiblioBazaar. Charlston 2009 (after the original dating from 1910).

Czekaj, Thomas; Stratmann, Vera; in Kooperation mit Holzapfel, Helmut et al.: Stadt und Kommunikation. Teilprojekt im Verbundprojekt EVALO – Eröffnung von Anpassungsfähigkeit für lebendige Orte. Verbundprojekt im Forschungsprogramm "Bauen und Wohnen im 21. Jahrhundert" des Bundesministeriums für Bildung und Forschung BMBF. Bremen 2004.

Davis, Mike: Eine Geschichte der Autobombe. Berlin/Hamburg 2007.

Der Spiegel: Tempo 20. Issue 34, pp. 24–34, 1963.

Die Zeit: Es war nur Totschlag. Issue 6/1966.

Divall, Colin; Bond, Winstan (eds.): Suburbanizing the masses; public transport and urban development in a historical perspective. Aldershot 2003.

Duden Fremdwörterbuch, 3rd edition. Mannheim 1974.

Durth, Werner: Die Inszenierung der Alltagswelt – zur Kritik der Stadtgestaltung. Braunschweig 1977.

Durth, Werner; Gutschow, Niels: Deutsche Architekten? Biographische Verflechtungen 1900–1970. München 1992.

Durth, Werner; Gutschow, Nils: Träume in Trümmern, Stadtplanung 1940–1950. München 1993.

Enzensberger, Hans Magnus: Vergebliche Brandung der Ferne. Eine Theorie des Tourismus. In: Merkur, 12th volume, 1958. Reprinted in: Universitas, 42nd volume, 1987, pp. 660–676.

EVALO (Verbundprojekt); Eröffnung von Anpassungsfähigkeit für lebendige Orte. Endbericht Gesamtprojekt. Published by: Brandt, Heike; Holzapfel, Helmut; Hopmeier, Ilka. Kassel 2004.

Fahlbusch, Michael: Deutschtumspolitik und westdeutsche Forschungsgemeinschaft. In: Dietz, Burckhard; Gabel, Hemut; Tiedau, Ulrich (eds.): Griff nach dem Westen. Die Forschung der völkisch-nationalen Wissenschaften zum nordwesteuropäischen Raum (1919–1960), Teil 2. Münster 2003.

Feldtkeller, Andreas: Die zweckentfremdete Stadt: Wider die Zerstörung des öffentlichen Raums. Frankfurt am Main 1994.

Feldtkeller, Andreas; Holzapfel, Helmut: Beiträge zu einem neuen Städtebau. Kassel 1999.

Flusser, Vilém: Kommunikalogie. Frankfurt am Main 1998.

Foucault, Michel: Die Heterotopien/Der utopische Körper. Zwei Radiovorträge. Frankfurt am Main 2005.

Frankfurter Allgemeine Zeitung, F.A.Z.: 50 Jahre Tempo 50. 3 July 2007, no. 151, p. T6.

Fraunholz, Uwe: Motorphobia. Göttingen 2002.

Gassner, Edmund: Die städtebauliche Infrastruktur. In: Pehnt, Wolfgang; Die Stadt in der Bundesrepublik. Lebensbedingungen, Anforderungen, Planung. Stuttgart 1974.

Gesenius, Wilhelm: Hebräisches und Aramäisches Handwörterbuch über das Alte Testament. 18th edition, 4th instalment. Berlin/Heidelberg 2007.

Graham, Stephen; Marvin, Simon: Splintering Urbanism. New York 2001.

Gröning, Gert; Wolschke-Bulmahn, Joachim: Der Drang nach Osten. Zur Entwicklung der Landespflege im Nationalsozialismus und während des zweiten Weltkrieges in den eingegliederten Ostgebieten. München 1987.

Gruen, Arno: Der Verrat am Selbst – Die Angst vor Autonomie bei Mann und Frau. München 1986.

Gutberlet, Bernd: Tempo! Wie das Auto die Welt verändert hat. Berlin 2007.

Habermas, Jürgen: Strukturwandel der Öffentlichkeit. Untersuchungen zu einer Kategorie der bürgerlichen Gesellschaft (Habil.). Neuwied 1962.

Hägerstrand, Torsten: "What about People in Regional Science?" Papers of the Regional Science Association vol. 24, 1970, pp. 7–21.

Hall, Peter: Cities in Civilization: Culture, Technology, and Urban Order. London/New York 1998.

Hegemann, Werner: Das steinerne Berlin (after the original version dating from 1930), Bauwelt-Fundamente 3. Berlin 1992.

Hoffmann-Axthelm, Dieter: Die dritte Stadt. Bausteine eines neuen Gründungsvertrags. Frankfurt am Main 1993.

Holzapfel, Helmut: Autonomie statt Auto – Zum Verhältnis von Lebensstil, Umwelt und Ökonomie am Beispiel des Verkehrs. Bonn 1997.

Holzapfel, Helmut (ed.): Ökologische Verkehrsplanung. Die Wechselwirkung von Raumerschließung und Raumzerstörung. Frankfurt am Main 1988.

Holzapfel, Helmut: Ökologen sollten gegen die Maut sein. In: Frankfurter Rundschau, 26 April 2010.

Holzapfel, Helmut: Ich lieb ihn sehr, den Kreisverkehr. In: AG Freiraum und Vegetation (pub.); Notizbuch 78 der Kasseler Schule – Altmark-Reise Ackerbrachen. Kassel 2010.

Holzapfel, Helmut: Verkehrsplanung in den "Neuen Bundesländern". Erfahrungen aus der Praxis. In: Altrock, Uwe et al. (eds.) Zwanzig Jahre Planung seit der Wiedervereinigung, Berlin 2010, pp. 315–324.

Holzapfel, Helmut; Traube, Klaus; Ulrich, Otto: Autoverkehr 2000. Karlsruhe 1985.

Holzapfel, Helmut; Sachs, Wolfgang: So verwandeln sich Lebensräume in bloße Verbindungswege. Ein Beitrag zur Automobilausstellung 1981. Frankfurter Rundschau issue no. 221, 24 September 1981.

Holz-Rau, Christian: Verkehr und Verkehrswissenschaft – Verkehrspolitische Herausforderungen aus Sicht der Verkehrswirtschaft In: Schwedes, Oliver: Verkehrspolitik. Eine interdisziplinäre Einführung. Wiesbaden 2011, pp. 115–139.

Huber, Felix: Zukunftsperspektiven und Innovationen im öffentlichen Verkehr. In: Internationales Verkehrswesen, issues 7+8, 2001.

Hülbusch, Karl Heinrich: Die Straße als Freiraum. In: Stadt und Grün, volume 25, issue 4, 1996.

Hülbusch, Inge Meta: Innenhaus und Außenhaus – umbauter sozialer Raum. Schriftenreihe der OE ASL, issue 33, Gh Kassel. Kassel 1978.

Illich, Ivan: Selbstbegrenzung. Reinbek 1975.

Isbary, Gerhard: Möglichkeiten der Neuordnung im ländlichen Raum. Lecture held at the 14th class of the Institut für Städtebau der Deutschen Akademie für Städtebau und Landesplanung "Aktuelle Planungsprobleme der Gemeinden", 11–15 October 1965 in Wiesbaden.

Jacobs, Allan B.: Great Streets. Cambridge, MA 1993.

Jacobs, Jane: Tod und Leben großer amerikanischer Städte. Bauwelt-Fundamente Bd.4. Braunschweig 1963.

Jencks, Charles: The language of post-modern architecture. New York 1977.

Jencks, Charles: Die Meta-Erzählung der Postmoderne. In: Flagge, Ingeborg; Schneider, Romana (eds.); Revision der Postmoderne. Publikation zur entsprechenden Ausstellung. Frankfurt 2004.

Joachimsthaler, Anton: Die Breitspurbahn, das Projekt zur Erschließung des groß-europäischen Raumes 1942–1945. München 1999.

Jones, Peter; Boujenko, Natalya: "Link" and "Place": A New Approach to Street Planning and Design, Paper presented to the 32nd Australasian Transport Research Forum Conference in Auckland, September 2009.

Kaltenbrunner, Robert: Expansionswahn, Frankfurter Rundschau, 13 July 2010.

Kenworthy, Jeffrey; Newman, Peter: Sustainability and Cities; Overcoming Automobile Dependence. Washington D.C. 1999.

Kenworthy, Jeffrey; Newman, Peter: Urban Design to Reduce Automobile Dependence. In: Opolis; An International Journal of Suburban and Metropolitan Studies, volume 2, issue 1, article 3, pp. 35–52, 2006.

Kettler, Dietmar: Grundrecht auf Mobilität? Die Mobilitätsbedürfnisse von Kindern und Jugendlichen im Recht. Berlin 2005.

Keuning Instituut, Senza Communicatie: Shared Space; Raum für alle. Groningen/Leeuwarden 2005.

Knoflacher, Hermann: Grundlagen der Verkehrs und Siedlungsplanung; Verkehrsplanung. Wien/Köln/Weimar 2007.

Krämer-Badoni, Thomas; Kuhm, Klaus: Die Gesellschaft und ihr Raum. Raum als Gegenstand der Soziologie. Opladen 2003.

Kruse, Lenelis: Räumliche Umwelt. Berlin/New York 1974.

Kuchenbuch, Ludolf (with the collaboration of Jean Robert): Lehrbrief 1 "Raum und Geschichte" der Fern Universität Hagen. Hagen 1997.

Kuhle, Dagmar; Protze, Käthe; Theiling, Christoph; Witzel, Norbert: Möglichkeiten für Lebensorte und Arbeitsorte. Teilprojekt im Verbundprojekt EVALO – Eröffnung von Anpassungsfähigkeit für lebendige Orte. Verbundprojekt im Forschungsprogramm "Bauen und Wohnen im 21. Jahrhundert" des Bundesministeriums für Bildung und Forschung BMBF. Bremen 2004.

Kutter, Eckhard: Mobilität als Determinante städtischer Lebensqualität. In: Beiträge zu Verkehr in Ballungsräumen. Annual conference of the DVWG (Deutsche Verkehrswissenschaftliche Gesellschaft – German Association of Transport Sciences) in Köln 1974. Berlin 1975.Lampugnani, Vittorio Magnago: Die Stadt im 20. Jahrhundert: Visionen, Entwürfe, Gebautes. Berlin 2010.

Läpple, Dieter: Essay über den Raum; für ein gesellschaftswissenschaftliches Raumkonzept. In: Stadt und Raum; soziologische Analysen (Reihe Stadt, Raum und Gesellschaft Bd. 1). Pfaffenweiler 1992.

Le Corbusier: An die Studenten – Die "Charte d'Athènes". Reinbek bei Hamburg 1962.

Lefèbvre, Henri: Die Revolution der Städte. München 1972.

Lefèbvre, Henri: The production of space. Oxford 2005.

Leinberger, Christopher B.: The option of urbanism. Washington 2007.

Lewin, Kurt: Der Richtungsbegriff in der Psychologie. Der spezielle und der allgemeine hodologische Raum. In: Psychische Forschung 19, 1934.

Linde, Hans: Sachdominanz in Sozialstrukturen. Tübingen 1983.

Lose, Dieter; Schiller, Christian; Teichert, Heidrun: Das Verkehrsnachfragemodell EVA – Simultane Verkehrserzeugung, Verkehrsverteilung und Verkehrsaufteilung. In: Straßenverkehrstechnik, volume 50, issue 4, 2006.

Lüken-Isberner, Folckert: Kassel – neue Stadt auf altem Grund. In: Beyme, Klaus von; Durth, Werner; Gutschow, Niels (eds.); Neue Städte aus Ruinen. Deutscher Städtebau der Nachkriegszeit. München 1992.

Marinetti, Filippo Tommaso: Manifest des Futurismus. In: Le Figaro. Paris 1909.

Monheim, Heiner: Die Autofixierung der Verkehrspolitik. In: Monheim, Heiner; Zöpel, Christoph (eds.); Raum für Zukunft. Zur Innovationsfähigkeit von Stadtentwicklungs und Verkehrspolitik. Essen 2008, pp. 324–340.

Mitscherlich, Alexander: Die Unwirtlichkeit unserer Städte – Anstiftung zum Unfrieden. Frankfurt am Main 1969.

Mumford, Lewis: Die Stadt. Geschichte und Ausblick. Köln 1963.

Papp, Alexander von: Achsen in der Raumordnungspolitik des Bundes – Überlegungen zur Präzisierung der Achsenkonzepte. In: Kistenmacher, H.: Zur Problematik von Entwicklungsachsen. Hannover 1976.

Petersen, Rudolf; Schallaböck, Karl-Otto: Mobilität für morgen. Berlin, Basel, Boston 1995.

Piggott, Stuart: Prehistoric India to 1000 B.C. Harmondsworth 1950.

Pörksen, Uwe: Weltmarkt der Bilder. Eine Philosophie der Visiotype. Stuttgart 1997.

Proshansky, Harold M.; Ittelson, William H.; Rifkin, Leanne G. (eds.): Environmental Psychology. People and their physical settings. New York 1970.

Protze, Käthe; Theiling, Christoph in cooperation with Holzapfel, Helmut: Lebenswerte Stadtquartiere. Report written on behalf of the Friedrich-Ebert-Stiftung (Friedrich-Ebert-Foundation). Bonn 2000.

Protze, Käthe: Hausen statt Wohnen. AG Freiraum und Vegetation (pub.): Notizbuch 74 der Kasseler Schule. Kassel 2009.

Reichhardt, Hans Joachim; Schäche, Wolfgang: Von Berlin nach Germania. Über die Zerstörung der Reichshauptstadt durch Albert Speers Neugestaltungsplanungen. Berlin 2008.

Reichow, Hans Bernhard: Organische Stadtbaukunst. Braunschweig 1948.

Reichow, Hans Bernhard: Die autogerechte Stadt. Ravensburg 1959.

Rekacewicz, Philippe: "Lunch lecture" at the documenta XII, Kassel, 4 September 2007.

Ronellenfitsch, Michael; Holzapfel, Helmut: Ist Mobilität ein menschliches Grundbedürfnis? Pro und Contra. In: ZEIT Punkte Magazin 3/2000, Bewegte Welt.

Ronneberger, Klaus: Vorlesungsmanuskripte zur Veranstaltung Gesellschaft und Umwelt. Universität Kassel 2010.

Sachs, Wolfgang; Holzapfel, Helmut: Automobilisierung und Ungleichheit. Berlin 1981.

Sachs, Wolfgang: Die Liebe zum Automobil. Ein Rückblick in die Geschichte unserer Wünsche. Reinbek bei Hamburg 1998.

Sammer, Gerd: Kostenwahrheit auf den Tisch! Zur Zukunft von Verkehr und Mobilität. IT's T.I.M.E. Technology. Innovation. Management. Engineering; issue 1; publisher: ARCS – Österreichisches Forschungszentrum Seibersdorf 2001, p. 77.

Sassen, Saskia: Metropolen des Weltmarktes. Frankfurt am Main/New York 2006.

Saunders, Doug: Arrival City – How the Largest Migration in History is Reshaping Our World. London 2011.

Schekahn, Anke: Landwirtschaft und Landschaftsplanung. Die Aufgaben der Landwirtschaft aus planerischer Sicht vom Anfang der Industriegesellschaft bis heute. Arbeitsberichte des Fachbereiches Stadtplanung, Landschaftsplanung, 128, Universität Gesamthochschule Kassel. Kassel 1998.

Schivelbusch, Wolfgang: Geschichte der Eisenbahnreise; Zur Industrialisierung von Raum und Zeit im 19.Jahrhundert. München/Wien 1977.

Schlögel, Karl: Reading Time through Space: On the History of Civilisation and Geo-Politics, Goethe   Foundation,   www.litrix.de/buecher/sachbuecher/jahr/2004/raumelesenzeit/ leseproben/enindex.htm (accessed 30 October 2014).

Schröteler von Brandt, Hildegard: Städtebau und Stadtplanungsgeschichte. Stuttgart 2008.

Sieverts, Thomas: Zwischenstadt. Zwischen Ort und Welt, Raum und Zeit, Stadt und Land. Braunschweig 1997.

Simmel, Georg: Brücke und Tür. Essays. Stuttgart 1957.

Sitte, Camillo: Der Städtebau nach seinen künstlerischen Grundsätzen. Basel 2002.

Sloterdijk, Peter: Im Weltinnenraum des Kapitals. Frankfurt am Main 2005.

Spiegel, Erika: Stadtstruktur und Gesellschaft. In: Zur Ordnung der Siedlungsstruktur. Hannover 1974.

Stadt Kassel – Der Magistrat; Dezernat für Bauwesen, in Zusammenarbeit mit dem Dezernat für Umwelt, Verkehr und Sport und der Kasseler Nahverkehrs-Gesellschaft (pub.): Zur Diskussion; Generalverkehrsplan. Kassel 1988.

Steierwald, Gerd, et al.: Stadtverkehrsplanung; Grundlagen, Methoden, Ziele. Berlin 2005.

Stichweh, Rudolf: Raum und moderne Gesellschaft. Aspekte der sozialen Kontrolle des Raums. In: Krämer-Badoni, Thomas; Kuhm, Klaus: Die Gesellschaft und ihr Raum. Raum als Gegenstand der Soziologie. Opladen 2003.

Strohkark, Ingrid: Die Wahrnehmung von "Landschaft" und der Bau von Autobahnen in Deutschland, Frankreich und Italien vor 1933. Berlin 2001.

Stübben, Josef: Der Städtebau. Handbuch für Architektur. Stuttgart 1890.

Thaler, Andreas; Winkler, Matthias: Die fragmentierte Region. In: Raumplanung 120/121, 2005.

Topp, Hartmut: Der Arbeitsprozess für das IVL und der Zeitplan. Lecture manuscript 2003.

Traube, Klaus: Müssen wir umschalten? Von den politischen Grenzen der Technik. Reinbek bei Hamburg 1983.

Tucholsky, Kurt: Gesammelte Werke 7. Reinbek bei Hamburg 1960.

Twickel, Christoph: Gentrifidingsbums oder eine Stadt für alle. Hamburg 2010.

Ullrich, Otto: Technik und Herrschaft. Frankfurt am Main 1977.

Van Laak, Dirk: Über alles in der Welt. Deutscher Imperialismus im 19 und 20. Jahrhundert. München 2005.

Verband Deutscher Verkehrsunternehmen (VDV – Association of German Public Transport Companies, pub.): VDV-Statistik 2012. Köln 2013.

Verkehrsclub Österreich (pub.): Soziale Aspekte von Mobilität. Wien 2009.

Veyne, Paul (ed.): Geschichte des privaten Lebens. 5 Bde., Bd.1, Vom Römischen Imperium zum Byzantinischen Reich. Frankfurt am Main 1989.

Vitruv: Baukunst 2.Band, Übersetzung A. Rode. Zürich/München 1987.

Volkswagen AG (pub.): Volkswagen entdecken – Ihr Reiseführer. Broschüre für Käufer der Marke Volkswagen. Wolfsburg (undated).

Weber, Max: Wirtschaft und Gesellschaft. Tübingen 1922.

Wendorff, Rudolf: Zeit und Kultur. Geschichte des Zeitbewußtseins in Europa. Opladen 1980.

Westermann, A.: Zukunft unserer Kinder – Wohnen in der Sackgasse. In: AG Freiraum und Vegetation (pub.); Die Boden-Rente ist sicher. Beiträge zur Organisation des Bau, Freiraum und Siedlungsgrundrisses. Notizbuch 56 der Kasseler Schule. Kassel 2000.

Whitelegg, John: Critical Mass: Transport Environment and Society in the Twenty-First Century. London 1997.

Winning, Hans-Henning V.: Entzauberung des Space of Flows – Sprit-Autos als Kraftwerke und andere Perspektiven, In: Ulf Hahne (ed.): Globale Krise – Regionale Nachhaltigkeit. Detmold 2010.

Zeh, Juli: Das Prinzip Gregor. In: Neue Gesellschaft, Frankfurter Hefte "Weg zum Glück", Bonn November 2010, pp. 20–23.

Zöpel, Christoph: Bilanz der Stadtentwicklung in Deutschland. In: Monheim, Heiner; Zöpel, Christoph (eds.) Raum für Zukunft. Zur Innovationsfähigkeit von Stadtentwicklungs und Verkehrspolitik. Essen 2008, pp. 501–503.

Zumkeller, Dirk: Prognosen der kommunalen Verkehrsplanung. In: Apel; Holzapfel; Kiepe; Lehmbrock; Müller (eds.); Handbuch der kommunalen Verkehrsplanung, 46. Ergänzungslieferung, Teil 3.2.3.1. Bonn 2007.

ACKNOWLEDGEMENTS

I would like to thank all those who helped me with their suggestions and assistance regarding the contents and translation of this book, namely Prof. Arno Gruen, Prof. Thomas Krämer-Badoni, Garth Pritchard (translation), and Swen Schneider (copyediting).

INDEX

f refers to figures and n refers to notes i.e., 59n48 indicates page 59, note 48.